HOW TO USE CONTINGENCY CONTRACTING IN THE CLASSROOM

"A child's mind is not a vessel to be filled, but a flame to be kindled."

—— Henry Steele Commager

How to Use Contingency Contracting in the Classroom

Revised Edition

Lloyd Homme

with Attila P. Csanyi
Mary Ann Gonzales
and James R. Rechs

Introduction by
Wesley C. Becker

Research Press
2612 N. Mattis Ave., Champaign, Ill. 61820

Much of the material in this book was developed and field tested under research grants from the United States Office of Education.

Eleventh printing 1979

Printed in the United States of America

Copies of this book may be ordered from Research Press at the address given on the title page.

ISBN 0-87822-050-X

CONTENTS

INTRODUCTION

Wesley C. Becker, Ph.D.
Bureau of Educational Research
University of Illinois

School failures do not "just happen." Like anything else, they have causes. For some time it has been customary to attribute school failure to such causes as "low intelligence," "poor motivation," "lack of interest," "emotional problems," "poor home life." Current research going on in public schools and experimental schools is convincingly demonstrating that school failures can be overcome by *better teaching programs* and the *effective use of positive reinforcement* to motivate children. In this book, the authors present one approach to the systematic use of reinforcement principles to motivate better learning–*contingency contracting.* The general procedure is deceptively simple: *arrange the conditions so that the child gets to do something he wants to do following something you want him to do.*

Contingency contracting in the hands of Lloyd Homme has an imaginative and humorous history. In 1963 he was faced with the task of controlling the behavior of three three-year-olds *without* using punishment or tangible reinforcers such as candy or trinkets. Lloyd Homme relates what happened:

"The amount of control exercised on the first day can be summarized: none. One child was running and screaming, another was pushing a chair across the floor (rather a noisy chair), and the other was playing with a jigsaw puzzle. Once our scholars discriminated that punishment did not follow these activities (the rate at which this discrimination was made must have set a new indoor record), the response to the verbal instruction 'Come and sit down now' was to continue the running and screaming, chair-pushing, and so forth . . . ."*(p. 33)

Almost in desperation Lloyd Homme tried to see if a principle set forth by the psychologist David Premack might be made to work with these children.

In brief, the idea is that any behavior which has a high probability of occurring at time X can be used to reinforce or strengthen any behavior which has a lower probability of occurring at time X. For example, Premack has shown that animals would learn to drink *more water* when water was constantly available, if drinking water gave them an opportunity to run (and running was not otherwise permitted). Running was being used to reinforce drinking water. Most psychologists in the past had only tried to do it the other way: restrict drinking, and use drinking to reinforce running. The beauty of this finding for the teacher is that in order to decide what can be used to reinforce children, she need only observe what they choose to do when given the opportunity and use this activity as the reinforcer.

Lloyd Homme was a good observer. He noted that his children loved to run and scream, push chairs, and play with puzzles. He continues his story:

"We made engaging in these behaviors contingent on the subjects' doing a small amount—very small at first—of whatever we wanted them to do. A typical early contingency was merely for them to sit quietly in chairs and look at the blackboard. This was followed almost immediately by the command, 'Everybody, run and scream, now.'" This kind of contingency management put us in immediate control of the situation. We were in control to the extent that we were able to teach everything in about one month that we could discover was ordinarily taught in first grade."*

From this beginning, Lloyd Homme went to work with teachers at many levels with many kinds of children who had failed (or more correctly, had not been taught). The methods and rules for implementing contingency contracting were learned by finding out what worked. The result is the present volume. A basic rule of behavior is taught in a down-to-earth way. *Behavior is strengthened or weakened depending on its consequences.* In contingency contracting, the consequences are usually some other behaviors a child might like to engage in. However, this does not exhaust the ways in which reinforcing consequences can be systematically introduced in the classroom. There are variations on the procedures which may be more appropriate to one classroom than another. For example, instead of immediately following an academic task with a reinforcing activity or event, the teacher might give the children points, stars, or tickets which can be exchanged at some *later time* for a reinforcer. Or the teacher could give notes which are taken home and exchanged by the parents for some reinforcing event. In other words, I would encourage the reader to learn well the basic lessons being taught in this manual, but then be imaginative in working out ways of adapting the procedures to your children and setting.

Urbana, Illinois, March, 1969

---

*Homme, Lloyd E. "Human motivation and environment," *Kansas Studies in Education,* Lawrence, Kansas, 1966, *16,* 30-39.

HOW TO USE THIS BOOK

Objectives. This book explains an extremely effective method of motivating elementary and high school students. The method, contingency contracting, is based on the systematic application of some generally accepted principles of human behavior. One of these principles is that a desired kind of behavior is more likely to recur if it is followed by some kind of reward each time it occurs.

Another underlying principle is that children can learn more willingly and satisfactorily if the framework within which learning takes place has been mutually agreed upon between teacher and student.

A teacher who uses contingency contracting makes an agreement or contract with his students under which he promises rewards in return for the desired learning behavior by the students. The method can be used at any grade level and with any subject. The method—or variations of it—has been applied successfully with normal children in regular public school classrooms, with children suffering from severe emotional disturbances, by parents within their own families, and in many other situations. As a matter of fact, the successes achieved with behavior management systems of this kind during the past few years have established it as one of the most significant developments of the twentieth century in applied psychology.

Who Can Use this Book. This book has been prepared primarily for the elementary or high school teacher. The educational background of the average teacher gives the prerequisites for understanding and using contingency contracting, regardless of the teacher's subject of specialization. The book assumes that the reader is somewhat familiar with the basics of individual instruction, and that the reader wants to employ systematic motivation management techniques in an individualized instructional setting. As a matter of fact, the only factor at all likely to interfere with application of the method by an experienced teacher would be an unwillingness to try new methods that depart from the normal classroom routine.

The Structure of Part I. Each of the five opening chapters of this book has three parts. The first part is a self-diagnostic pretest covering the section's content. If the reader can pass this pretest and the corresponding post-test, he is directed to the pretest of the next chapter, because there is no need for him to go through all the intervening material.

The second part of each chapter consists of a narrative summary, with a corresponding intermediate diagnostic test. Most readers will find that they can pass a number of these tests, after reading the summary sections. If so, the reader is directed to the next section of the chapter.

The third section is presented in the form of a sequence of small statement-and-question steps, called frames. This frame sequence will clarify any points of the content which might have been left unclear to the reader by the summary. It will amplify points of the summary by examples, definitions, and explanations. By means of these "exercises" and the post-test, the reader can be sure that he has acquired full understanding and mastery of the material before he goes on the next chapter.

Answers to the pre-, intermediate, and post-tests of each section are given in the back of the book, with instructions on where to go next, based on the reader's self-evaluation of his answers.

The Criterion Test. Upon completion of the sixth chapter, the reader should take the self-diagnostic criterion test. The answers to the criterion test, given in the back of the book, are referenced to corresponding source passages in Part I. They provide an opportunity for quick review of "weak" areas.

Structure of Part II. Because the content of the second part of the book is more concrete, a different form of programing is used. First a small amount of information is presented in straight expository form. Then a brief series of questions is given, based on the preceding paragraphs. These questions function in the same way as both the intermediate tests and the instructional frames in Part I. If you miss any of the questions, reread the section that precedes it.

When you have accurately completed all the paragraphs and questions in a chapter, you are ready for the post-test of that chapter. At the end of the book is a criterion test on the entire content of Part II. A perfect or nearly perfect score on this test should indicate that the reader has a full understanding of contingency management and is ready to establish a contract system in an actual classroom.

PART I

HOW CONTINGENCY CONTRACTING WORKS

1

"Something pleasant will happen if . . ."

Pretest

Directions: Place a check mark by each choice you think is correct. All or none (both or neither) may be correct for any one item. (You are not expected to be able to answer these questions unless you are already familiar with the material covered in this section.)

1. Which of these would be an example of a **positive contingency contract?**

____ a. "If you perform something which is desirable to me, I will in turn provide something which is desirable to you."
____ b. "If you want to avoid punishment, you must perform such and such a task."

2. In everyday life, positive contingency contracts are most frequently applied in

____ a. business relations.
____ b. friendships.
____ c. criminal law.

3. Positive contingency contracts are

____ a. rarely used in ordinary educational situations.
____ b. rarely used in everyday family situations.

Match your answers against the answers given on page 119.

Summary

One of the major problems educators and parents have faced throughout the ages has been that of motivating children to perform tasks, whose desirability was determined by these adults.

Traditionally, **negative contingencies** have been favored to achieve this goal. In other words, the adult imposes a kind of "contract." The contract in such cases is: "In order to avoid punishment, you must perform such and such a task." The method advocated in this book is, on the other hand, a method of positive contingencies. The contract in this case takes the form: "As soon as you demonstrate that you have learned a little more, you may do something which is even more enjoyable."

Contracts of the latter kind are used every day, most obviously in the world of commercial and business enterprises. When one goes shopping, takes a job, or hires an employee, positive contingency contracts are implicit. In fact, with the exception of the legal system, whose approach is basically negative[1], our everyday life is largely run by positive contracts. Wherever such contracts meet the criteria of fairness and honesty, they fill important needs as bases for interpersonal relations. The purpose of this book is to make the rules of contingency contracting explicit to those who work with people every day, especially those who work with children.

The principles and rules of positive contingency contracts can be used for the management of relationships between teachers and the children they are handling. Though the majority of parents and educators have, in fact, used these rules for countless generations, they have not been explicitly stated, nor have they been used consistently or systematically. This book specifies these rules, shows their relationship to sound principles of behavioral science, and shows how they apply to the management of motivation in the school and in the home. The ultimate objective of behavioral motivation technology is shifting to self-management, so that the individual assumes responsibility for motivating his own behavior. (See Chapter 5.)

The reason for bringing up the "ultimate objectives" at this time is to reassure those teachers who may be dubious about the whole idea of motivation management. They may be saying

---

1 For example: "If you do not violate the law, you will not be punished." This statement can be converted into: "If you do violate the law, you will be punished," by removing the negatives from both sides. It does not, however, convert into "If you obey the law, you will be rewarded." This positive contract is neither implied logically, nor practiced in reality in criminal law.

to themselves, "Students should be motivated by a desire to succeed, not by the promise of a reward," or "This sounds like bribery to me." Or the teacher may be thinking, "If I apply contingency contracting systematically now, won't the child grow up expecting rewards for every little thing he does?" Although the writers of this program had similar concerns in the past, experiences have proven otherwise. Children who participate in a program of systematic contingency management turn out to be happy, eager-to-learn children for whom learning itself becomes one of the most rewarding experiences.

Intermediate Test

Directions: In each sentence, circle one of the two words in italics.

1. In business relations, the agreements made between client and businessman, employer and employee, seller and buyer are normally examples of *positive/negative* contingency contracts.

2. "To avoid punishment, do as I tell you," is an example of a *positive/negative* contingency contract.

3. Traditionally, *positive/negative* contingencies have been favored to achieve the goals of motivating children.

Match your answers against the answers given on page 119.

Instructional Frames

Directions: Use an envelope or folded piece of paper to mask the answer column at the right-hand edge of the page. Then read each question and mark your choice of an answer. You can select all or none of the alternative answers given. Move the mask down to reveal the correct answer. If your answer is correct, proceed to the next frame; if not, reread the question so that you understand why the answer given is correct.

1. Educational objectives are accomplished by **learning**. Learning comes about through **performance**. In order to perform, any human being, including the student, must be **motivated**. Thus, the fundamental tasks of the teacher should include

____ a. determining educational objectives.
____ b. motivating student performance.
____ c. guiding student performance.

a, b and c

2. Motivation, as such, is nearly always present in any human being. Motivation can also be induced–that is, artificially created. Induced motivation is most commonly created by some form of threat. Motivation, in this case, results in performance by the individual in order to

____ a. achieve some goal.
____ b. escape the threatened punishment. b

3. The consequences of the performance of a student under motivation may be

____ a. the attainment of some highly desired goal.
____ b. escape from a threatened punishment. a and b

4. The consequences of an act performed under motivation are called the *contingencies* of this act. We may speak of both **positive** and **negative contingencies.** Negative contingencies would be found under the condition of

____ a. induced motivation.
____ b. threat of punishment. a and b

5. "I'll spank you unless you perform such and such a task." This is an example of

____ a. natural (as opposed to induced) motivation.
____ b. a positive contingency. neither

6. "If you perform something desirable to me, I will in turn provide something which you desire." This is an example of

____ a. a positive contingency.
____ b. a negative contingency. a

7. The kind of agreement described in the previous two frames, either positive or negative, is a kind of contract. The term used for presenting such a contract is **contingency contracting**. Which is an example of contingency contracting?

____ a. "Here's $10. Go buy yourself a present."
____ b. "Get all of the next ten problems correct and you may watch this 10-minute movie cartoon." b

8. Contingency contracting can be

___ a. positive.
___ b. negative.

a and b

9. When a mother says to her child, "As soon as you pick up your toys, you may go outside," this is an example of ______________ contingency contracting.

positive

10. Making an agreement with someone, in which an outcome is made dependent upon performance, is called ______________ ______________.

contingency contracting

11. When a person, by his performance, avoids some threatening situation, we speak of (a) __________ (positive/negative) contingency contracting. When, on the other hand, performance results in achieving something desirable to the performer, we call it a (b) ____________ (positive/negative) contract.

a. negative
b. positive

12. Positive contracts may be explicit (formally stated) or implicit (not formally expressed). When a company rewards an employe for some accomplishment with an unexpected bonus, this is an example of an (a) __________(implicit/explicit) contract. On the other hand, the money he receives for a month's work is an example of being rewarded under an (b) ____________ (implicit/explicit) contract.

a. implicit
b. explicit

13. Under law, you are forbidden to cross an intersection on a red signal light. Among other things, the motivation for stopping at a red light is related to the fact that

___ a. stopping will be rewarded by the police department.
___ b. stopping will prevent punishment by the police department.

b

14. One example of a business transaction is the operation of vending machines. The motivation for placing a dime into a soft drink machine is related to the fact that

____ a. the act is rewarded by the soft drink you obtain.
____ b. it prevents punishment by the soft drink company.

a

15. In general, business transactions involve (a) ______________ contingency contracts, while obeying the law involves (b) ______________ contingency contracts.

a. positive
b. negative

Post-test

1. For a contingency contract to be positive, the terms offered in it must imply

____ a. a reward.
____ b. an opportunity to avoid punishment.

2. "If you work 40 hours a week, you will be paid $100." This is an example of

____ a. an implicit negative contract.
____ b. an explicit positive contract.
____ c. an implicit positive contract.
____ d. an explicit negative contract.

3. A negative contingency contract might state

____ a. "If you don't do your homework this week, you will all get F's."
____ b. "If you eat your spinach, I will not spank you."

Match your answers against the answers given on page 119.

2

What makes a reinforcer work?

Pretest

1. To be worthwhile in a contingency contract, the reward offered must be

____ a. highly desirable.
____ b. not obtainable outside the contingency of the contract.

2. The reward in the contract must

____ a. increase the probability that the rewarded activity will recur.
____ b. maintain a high probability of the rewarded activity.
____ c. decrease the probability of the rewarded activity.

3. Reinforcing events may occur as

____ a. reinforcing stimuli.
____ b. reinforcing responses.
____ c. reinforcing stimuli and reinforcing responses combined.

Match your answers against the answers given on page 120.

Summary

In order to be worthwhile, the terms of a contingency contract must offer as a reward an experience which is (a) highly desirable and (b) not obtainable outside the conditions of the contract. If the terms on the student's side of the contract lead to such experiences, this will have one of two important effects: it will increase the probability that the students will perform the same activity in the future, or it will maintain in strength a behavior which is already strong. This will be true as long as the terms of the contract hold, and as long as the characteristics of desirability and attainability of the experience do not change. Of course, if the experience offered becomes less desirable, as it often does with time, or if the same experience will become attainable in other (easier) ways, the experience will lose its potential of having an effect on the student's performance. This characterization equates the experience offered in the contract with what is technically known as a **reinforcer.** A reinforcer in psychology is an event which, when it follows certain activities, increases the likelihood that these activities will recur.

Kinds of Reinforcers. There are many different kinds of reinforcers. Some reinforcers are characterized by the fact that they make it possible for an organism to engage himself in some desired *activity.* A person is more likely to perform a relatively boring and uninteresting task if the payoff is the opportunity to do something more interesting and entertaining. For example, fighting one's way through miles of holiday traffic is in itself not a very rewarding task. Still, thousands do this in order to visit relatives or friends. These kinds of reinforcers, called **reinforcing responses**, are things one *does,* or likes to do.

Other reinforcers involve things that *happen to* someone. For example, on a camping trip, a man may exert a great amount of energy to chop wood and create a camp fire (task), especially if the weather is chilly. Getting warm by the fire (which happens to the person) will, in this case, serve as a reinforcer. Technically, reinforcing events of this case are called **reinforcing stimuli.**

In summary, several kinds of reinforcers can be found. In this book, the phrase **reinforcing event** is used rather than the more conventional "reinforcing stimulus" to refer to all of these. A reinforcer is sometimes most conveniently characterized by its stimulus characteristics. "Very good," as a stimulus, clearly functions as a reinforcer, regardless of our inability to specify what behavior it elicits. But sometimes a reinforcer is most conveniently characterized by its response characteristics. Sometimes both a reinforcer's stimulus and response properties are apparent. For example, the stimulus, "Let's play a game," together with the complex of stimuli and responses involved in playing the game, are all part of the reinforcement. The phrase "reinforcing event" is broad enough to include all of these possibilities.

Intermediate Test

Directions: Mark each choice you think is correct. If the question has a missing word, write it in the space provided.

1. A reinforcer is

___ a. the same as a reward in a contingency contract.
___ b. something which, when it follows some act, will make that act more likely to be repeated.

2. Which of these is most conveniently characterized as a reinforcing *response?*

___ a. John writes a letter to Mary. Mary answers by calling John on the telephone.
___ b. John's boss agrees that if John puts in overtime during the week, he may take Friday afternoon off to go fishing for the weekend.

3. Which of these is most conveniently characterized as a reinforcing *stimulus?*

___ a. The cool air from an air conditioner on a hot day.
___ b. Playing with crayons.

4. The last four answers above (2 a, b, and 3 a, b) all have one property in common; they all involve reinforcing_________________.

Match your answers against the answers given on page 120.

Instructional Frames

1. A child will be likely to engage in some academic activity in order to be able to play with a particular toy as a reward, if he

___ a. finds playing with that toy highly desirable.
___ b. knows that this is the only way he can play with that particular toy. a and b

2. The desirability of a reward, *as indicated by the child,* will define it as a **potential reinforcer.** Which of the following is the best potential reinforcer?

___ a. Something the child says he would like to do or experience.

___ b. Something the child never experienced but selects from a list.

a

3. The characteristic of not being obtainable outside the conditions of a contract defines the reward as a **controlled reinforcer.** A controlled reinforcer is one which may occur

___ a. under various situations, as a consequence of many different kinds of activity.

___ b. only as a consequence of performing a particular act or sequence of acts.

b

4. The effect of being rewarded by a controlled reinforcer will be that the student will be more likely to repeat the same activity in the future. Which of the following would most likely be repeated?

___ a. The student does his homework in mathematics, and takes it to school the next day. In school, the teacher does not ask the students to turn in their homework.

___ b. Johnny's friend rings the doorbell, and asks if Johnny can come out and play. His mother says, "Yes, Johnny may go out after he finishes his homework." Johnny does his homework and then goes out to play with his friend.

b

5. In order to serve as a reinforcer, the reward offered in the contract must increase or maintain the probability of recurrence of the rewarded activity. Jim's reading behavior is weak. If his reading of a passage from his textbook is rewarded by some candy, but his reading activity does not increase in the future, this means that

___ a. Jim does not like candy.

___ b. candy is not a reinforcer for Jim in this particular situation.

b

6. In order for a reinforcer to remain strong, it must retain its characteristics of desirability and obtainability. In which of the following cases would it be unlikely for a previously working reward to maintain the activity?

___ a. The student no longer wants that particular reward.

___ b. The student is able to obtain that reward in other, easier ways.

a and b

7. By definition, a reinforcer is characterized by what it does to an organism's behavior. The most important characteristic of a reinforcer is that when an individual does something, and his activity is *followed* by the reinforcer, the chances will increase that he will repeat that activity again. This means that

___ a. a reinforcer should always precede the desired activity.

___ b. we know that a reinforcer is a reinforcer by seeing what happens after its administration.

b

8. The reinforcer has been traditionally referred to as a "reinforcing stimulus." In this course we speak of **reinforcing events.** A possible reason for this is

___ a. that not all reinforcers are easily characterized as stimuli.

___ b. that some reinforcers are more easily characterized as responses than as stimuli.

a and b

9. When the student chooses an opportunity to run around the school yard as a reward for some performance, this is an example of

___ a. a reinforcing response.

___ b. a reinforcing event.

a and b

10. When the student chooses a 10-minute movie cartoon as a reinforcer, this is an example of

___ a. a reinforcing response.

___ b. a reinforcing event.

b

11. Although all reinforcements have both response and stimulus characteristics, some are more easily characterized by their stimulus characteristics. These are referred to in this program as

___ a. reinforcing stimuli.
___ b. reinforcing responses.

a

12. Those reinforcers which are characterized more easily by their response properties are referred to in this program as

___ a. reinforcing responses.
___ b. reinforcing events.

a and b

13. The phrase "reinforcing event" may refer to reinforcers which can be characterized as (a)_______________ _______________ or (b)_______________ _______________.

a. reinforcing stimuli
b. reinforcing responses

14. Regardless of whether a reinforcer is best characterized by its stimulus or its response properties, its desirability as an otherwise unobtainable opportunity makes it a reinforcing event. A good way of finding out whether a reinforcer is desirable to a student is by

___ a. asking the student.
___ b. trying it as a reinforcer to see if it will make the performance it rewards recur.

a and b

15. Both reinforcing stimuli and reinforcing responses can be considered as _______________ _______________.

reinforcing events

16. The most important characteristic of a reinforcer is that it _______________ the probability that the response it follows will be repeated.

increases

17. In order for a reinforcer to remain a reinforcer, it must remain (a) _______________ to the student, and it must remain (b)_______________ in other ways.

a. desirable
b. unobtainable

Post-test

1. The reward offered in a contingency contract is likely to be effective

____ a. if it is highly desirable.
____ b. if it cannot be obtained outside the conditions of the contract.
____ c. only if it is a reinforcing stimulus.

2. An event which, when it follows an act of behavior, increases the likelihood that the act will be repeated, is technically known as a ________________.

3. A reward which enables one to engage in some desired activity is called a reinforcing ________________.

4. A reward which exposes one to a desirable environmental condition is technically known as a reinforcing ________________.

Match your answers against the answers given on page 120.

3

Grandma's Law and other rules

Pretest

1. The rules of contracting state that the contracting procedure should be

____ a. fair.
____ b. clear.
____ c. honest.
____ d. negative or positive.
____ e. positive only.
____ f. occasional.
____ g. systematic.

2. The contract should be arranged to reward the student

____ a. for obedience.
____ b. for accomplishment.
____ c. for proficiency from the start.
____ d. for small approximations.
____ e. before the performance.
____ f. after the performance.
____ g. immediately after the performance.
____ h. occasionally, with large amounts.
____ i. frequently, with small amounts.

Match your answers against the answers given on page 121.

Summary

As stated in Chapter 1, rules of contracting are not entirely unknown to the average teacher or parent. In fact, much of contingency contracting may be summed up in Grandma's Law, which states: "First clean up your plate, then you may have your dessert."

More formally and precisely, we can identify ten basic rules. The first five refer to the use of the reward in contracting, while the last five describe characteristics of proper contracting.

Rule 1. The contract payoff (reward) should be immediate. It is of particular importance that this rule be observed early in the game when the child is just learning about contracting. Initial contracts (see Rule 2) should demand a small bit of behavior, then a progress check to see whether the behavior was executed to the contractor's specifications. Then the reward should be offered *immediately*. It is important that the presentation of the reinforcer be contingent *only* on the adequate performance of the behavior and not, for example, on the passage of time. Contracting will go well to the extent that the precision of the performance-reward relationship is respected.

Rule 2. Initial contracts should call for and reward small approximations. If the initial performance requested from the student is a *small, simple-to-perform* approximation to the final performance desired, no difficulties will be encountered. If, on the other hand, the performance requested is too precise, and too difficult for the student to perform, no amount of reward will help. In fact, the major thing wrong with intuitive contingency contracting (as it sometimes occurs in everyday situations–see Grandma's Law above) is that the intuitive contingency manager does not settle for small steps or approximations. The intuitive contract is likely to say, "Clean your room," rather than, "First, put your shoes in the closet." The intuitive contingency contract is likely to say, "Do all the arithmetic problems at the end of the chapter correctly, then you may watch a movie." The systematic motivation manager is more likely to say, "Do the first two problems correctly, then we will watch a movie for five minutes." The employer, when he is training a new employe, always has to reward approximations. If the new employe were to be rewarded only for expert performance at the start, he would never obtain the offered reward and would more than likely void the contract (i.e., leave the job).

Rule 3. Reward frequently with small amounts. Experience has shown (and there is considerable laboratory evidence to support this) that it is far more effective to give frequent, small reinforcements than a few large ones. As Rule 2 indicates, this is of particular importance early in the game.

Rule 4. The contract should call for and reward accomplishment rather than obedience. Thus, the contract should say: "If you accomplish such and such, you will be rewarded with such and such," not, "If you do what I tell you to do, I will reward you with such and such." Reward for accomplishment leads to independence. Reward for obedience leads only to continued dependence on the person to whom the child learns to be obedient.

Rule 5. Reward the performance after it occurs. At first glance, this is the most self-evident of all the rules: first some task behavior, then some reinforcing responses or reinforcing stimuli. The reader may be saying to himself by now, "Why, that's nothing but the old 'first work, then play' rule." This is correct. But this book suggests that the rule must be taken much more seriously than is usually the case. The difference in contingency management is that the "first work, then play" sequence does not occur just once, twice, or three times a day. The task and the reinforcing events are broken down into small components, so that the sequence will occur dozens of times each day.

It is striking to note, when one begins to observe the *order* of events, how frequently the order is reversed. For example, "Just one more game of cards" (a reinforcing activity), "then you've *got* to do your homework" (a task event). Or, "Stop watching television" (a reinforcing event), "and carry out this trash" (a task event). The examples illustrate that these events do not, by themselves, automatically get broken down into small units and arranged in the correct order. That is the purpose of this book, to demonstrate the method of correctly managing contingencies.

Rule 6. The contract must be fair. This rule simply means that the terms of the contract, on both sides of the agreement ("If you will do X, I will do Y"), must be of relatively equal weight. Imagine a contract, for example, in which a teacher says to the student, "If you get all A's throughout the school year, I will take you to the movies." This kind of a contract could hardly be called fair. On the other hand, the teacher's saying, "If you sit quietly for two minutes, I will take you to the movies," would also be an unbalanced contract. In this case, the weight of what is offered by the initiator of the contract would be immensely greater than the weight of the behavior demanded by the contract. In general, one must try to relate the amount of reward to the amount of performance.

Teachers (and parents) sometimes feel uncomfortable with rewarding the students "for what they should be doing anyway." It seems to be somehow immoral to reward today's child for doing assignments that earlier generations had to do "or else." But the fact is that children learn better, and more willingly, if reinforcers follow difficult activities. We wouldn't say today's children should not get better dental care than their parents had. All schools provide some activities and objects for their children primarily because of their fun value. The crucial difference is in the time sequence of offering them.

Rule 7. The terms of the contract must be clear. This means that the terms on both sides of the agreement must be explicitly stated. For example, an unclear contract would say, "Do a few arithmetic problems and then we will do something more interesting." A more clearly stated contract would say, "Do ten arithmetic problems correctly and then we will watch the first four minutes of this Popeye cartoon." The child must always know *how much* performance is expected of him and *what he can expect as a payoff.*

Rule 8. The contract must be honest. An honest contract is one which is (a) carried out immediately, and (b) carried out according to the terms specified in the contract.

Rule 9. The contract must be positive. An appropriate contract should *not* say, "I will not do X, if you will do Y." The terms of the contract should *contribute* something to the child's experience, rather than take something away from him. Note that often contracts used in the school and in the home are implicitly of a negative type. E.g., "Behave as I tell you" implies "You will not get punished if you behave as I tell you." The outstanding characteristic of negative contracting is that it involves a threat of punishment.

Rule 10. Contracting as a method must be used systematically. Perhaps the most difficult thing to learn about the laws of contingency is that they go on working all the time, whether one pays any attention to them or not. That is to say, these laws do not hold only during arithmetic period or the reading lesson, or only during school hours, for that matter. A reinforcement following a bit of behavior will strengthen that behavior whether or not it occurs during school hours. As one becomes familiar with contingency management procedures one might ask, "What is the payoff for the child?" for almost every behavior requested of the child.

Once contracting has been established as a motivation-management procedure, it should be maintained, and care should be taken not to reward undesirable acts. Remember, the best way to eliminate unwanted behaviors is to make certain that they are *never* reinforced in any way; instead, see to it that in the same situation some other behavior *is* reinforced, which is itself incompatible with the undesirable behavior.

What is the payoff for the parent or teacher? The parents and teachers now using these rules in their management of child motivation find that children are eager to perform under these conditions. These children do not show the timid or aggressive traits of children performing under duress and coercion. Nor do they exhibit the demanding and "spoiled" characteristics of those who are used to receiving unearned benefits. There is a kind of joy in their activities; they seem to have a feeling of delight in their willing and conscious accomplishment and their well deserved rewards. Observing and participating in this kind of learning is, in turn, the greatest reward teachers or parents can experience.

Intermediate Test

1. Which of the following is (are) *not* consistent with the rules of contracting presented in this chapter?

___ a. "If you do 50 pushups, I'll give you an M&M candy."
___ b. "If you do a few pushups, I'll give you some candy."
___ c. "If you stop crying, I will not punish you."
___ d. "If you are obedient, I will reward you."

2. The student beginning a contract should be rewarded for

____ a. anything he does.
____ b. any small step which is an approximation of the desired performance.
____ c. only the most proficient performance.

3. The reward should be

____ a. given immediately after the performance has occurred.
____ b. matched to the amount of performance desired.
____ c. given frequently, in small amounts.

Match your answers against the answers given on page 121.

Instructional Frames

1. The first rule about using rewards in contracting is that the reward should be *immediate.* This means that

____ a. there should be a moderate time lapse between the occurrence of the task event and the occurrence of the reinforcing event.
____ b. the amount of time elapsed between the occurrence of the task event and the occurrence of the reinforcing event should approximate zero. — b

2. The first rule of contracting is that the reinforcing event should follow the task event ____________________ . — immediately

3. The first five rules of contracting refer to the way reinforcement should be used in contingency contracts. The second of these rules is that initial contracts should call for small approximations. This means that

____ a. on the first occasion, expert performance of a small task should be demanded.
____ b. on the first occasion, any small approximation to a desired response should be reinforced. — b

4. Which of the following examples is most consistent with the *small approximation* rule?

____ a. "Eat your dinner, then you may have dessert."
____ b. "Eat a spoonful of peas, then you may have a bite of your favorite meat."

b

5. Which of the following is an example of the use of small approximations?

____ a. "*Wanted.* Specialist in selling fire insurance. At least 4 years experience required."
____ b. "*Wanted.* Man willing to be trained as fire insurance salesman. Salary during training. Some selling background necessary."

b

6. The rule of small approximations requires that

____ a. any behavior should be reinforced in the beginning
____ b. in the beginning, any behavior that approximates the desired behavior should be reinforced.

b

7. The third rule of contracting is that the rewards should occur frequently in small amounts. Frequent reward is more likely to maintain the performance at high strength. For this reason, the activity that is rewarded more frequently is

____ a. more likely to be sustained for a long period of time.
____ b. less likely to be sustained for a long period of time.

a

8. The first three rules about rewards are that they should follow the behavior (a) ______________, they should be given for small (b) ______________, and they should be given (c) ______________.

a. immediately
b. approximations
c. frequently

9. The next rule of contracting is that the contract should call for *accomplishments* rather than obedience. This rule is exemplified by:

____ a. "If you accomplish such and such, you will be rewarded with such and such."
____ b. "If you do what I tell you to do, I will reward you with such and such."

a

10. The behavior and decisions of the child who is rewarded for obedience are likely to become increasingly

____ a. independent of the contingency manager.
____ b. dependent on the contingency manager.

b

11. "If you study and pass this quiz you will receive a free ticket to a movie you choose." This is an example of a contract calling for

____ a. accomplishment.
____ b. obedience.

a

12. In contingency contracting, the rules call for reinforcing (a)____________________ rather than (b)____________________, and for reinforcing (c)__________ ____________________ in the beginning.

a. accomplishment
b. obedience
c. small approximations

13. The fifth rule of contingency contracting states that a reinforcer should be presented *after* the performance occurs. This means that, in general, the procedure should be

____ a. first performance, then reinforcement.
____ b. first reinforcement, then performance.

a

14. The "reinforcement after performance" rule is the same as the old "first work, then play" rule. The major difference is that in contingency contracting the frequency of "work-then-play" events is enormously increased. In contingency contracting, therefore,

____ a. once in awhile, after a great amount of performance, the student should be rewarded by a great amount of reinforcement.

____ b. before small amounts of performance the student should be rewarded by small amounts of reinforcement, frequently.

neither

15. Which of the following is *not* consistent with the "reward after performance" rule?

____ a. "First I will go outside and play, then I will come back and do my homework."

____ b. "First I will do my homework, then I will go outside and play."

a

16. The sixth rule, which is the first rule about contracting itself, is that the contract must be *fair.* This means that

____ a. the contract must be fair to the parent or teacher initiating the contract.

____ b. the contract must be fair to the child.

a and b

17. In reality, an unfair contract has disadvantages for both parties. If a seller were to offer a loaf of bread for $100, this contract would be

____ a. unfair to the buyer.

____ b. disadvantageous to the seller. (The seller could not find anyone to contract for the bread, i.e., he could not sell it.)

a and b

18. Which of the following do you think would be the fairest contract with a second-grader?

___ a. "Read five pages of this text, complete the progress test, and if you pass you may play a game."
___ b. "Read 50 pages of this text, complete the progress test, and if you pass you may play a game."
___ c. "Read one sentence of this text, complete the progress test, and if you pass you may play a game."

a

19. The rule of contracting referred to is that the contract should be ____________________.

fair

20. Another rule is that the terms of the contract must be *clear*–that the terms of the contract must be *explicitly stated.* Which of the following would illustrate a clear contract?

___ a. "Read for awhile, then you can play ball for a few minutes."
___ b. "Read for awhile, then you can play ball for five minutes."
___ c. "Read five pages, then you can play ball for a few minutes."
___ d. "Read five pages, then you can play ball for five minutes."

d

21. The amount of work required and the amount of the payoff should always be clear.

a. In which of the examples in frame 20 was the amount of work unclear? _____
b. In which of the examples in frame 20 was the amount of payoff unclear? ______

a. a, b
b. a, c

22. Another rule of contracting is that the contract must be honest. An honest contract is defined as one which is

___ a. carried out immediately.
___ b. carried out according to the terms specified in the contract.

a and b

23. In an honest contract, therefore,

____ a. the reward may be delayed to some extent.
____ b. the terms of the contract may be changed after performance has occurred.

neither

24. In a particular contract, the teacher agrees to reward the class for good behavior by taking the class to the movies Friday afternoon. On Friday, the teacher who has made this agreement stays at home. From the point of view of the contract, this is

____ a. an honest contract.
____ b. a dishonest contract.

b

25. A language teacher makes a contract with her class. If they perform well during the month of December, she will organize a New Year's Ball for them, with a local pop orchestra providing the music. After the students perform according to contract during the month, there is only hi-fi music available at the New Year's Ball. This contract is (a)______________, because it is not (b)______________________________.

a. dishonest
b. carried out according to the terms stated

26. The first three rules of contracting are that the contract must be:

a. f____________________,
b. c____________________, and
c. h____________________.

a. fair
b. clear
c. honest

27. The next rule of contracting is that the contract must be *positive.* Chapter 1 of this book discussed the differences between positive and negative contingencies. You may infer that a positive contract is one which uses____________________ contingencies.

positive

28. The formula for a positive contingency contract is:

____ a. "I will not do X, if you will do Y."
____ b. "I will do X, if you will not do Y." — neither

29. In most everyday situations, "Behave as I tell you" implies

____ a. "You will not get punished if you behave as I tell you."
____ b. a negative contract. — a and b

30. The outstanding characteristic of negative contracting is that it involves

____ a. punishment.
____ b. the threat of punishment. — b

31. The formula for a positive contingency contract is "________________________." — "I will do X if you will do Y."

32. The last rule of contingency contracting is that contracting as a method must be used systematically. The teacher must remember that the child will consistently engage in some activity only if he knows that there is a rewarding payoff. The questions to be asked by the teacher are:

____ a. "What do I want the child to do?"
____ b. "How will I get him to do it?"
____ c. "What will be his payoff for doing it?" — a, b, c

33. Inconsistent use of contingency contracting may lead to reinforcing undesirable acts. By the nature of reinforcement, if an undesirable act is followed by a reinforcer,

____ a. it will tend to recur.
____ b. it will tend to disappear. — a

34. There is one way to treat undesirable acts that is consistent with contingency contracting. This is to *never* reinforce undesirable acts, but instead to reinforce some other, acceptable behavior, which cannot occur at the same time as (is incompatible with) the undesirable behavior. Therefore, to handle undesirable acts positively under this system,

____ a. undesirable acts should be punished.
____ b. undesirable acts should not be reinforced.
____ c. some desirable behavior should be reinforced which is incompatible with the undesirable act.

b, c

35. The ten rules of contingency contracting can be divided into two groups of rules. These are

____ a. rules about contracting and rules about the use of reinforcers in contracting.
____ b. rules about contracts and rules about reinforcement.

a

36. The last five rules of contingency contracting deal with________________ itself.

contracting

37. The last five rules state that the contract should be (a) f______ (b) c__________, (c)h___________, (d) p_______________, and contracting should be used (e) s______________________.

a. fair
b. clear
c. honest
d. positive
e. systematically

38. The first five rules deal with how to use ______________________ in contracting.

reinforcers

39. The contract should call for (a) a______________, rather than (b) o_______________.

a. accomplishment
b. obedience

40. Initially, the contract should call for __________ ______________________.

small approximations

41. The performance should be rewarded ____________ ________ it occurs.

immediately
after

Post-test

1. From memory, list the five most important characteristics of a contingency contract.

a. ____________________
b. ____________________
c. ____________________
d. ____________________
e. ____________________

2. List key words of the first five rules, regarding reward in contingency contracting.

a. ____________________
b. ____________________
c. ____________________
d. ____________________
e. ____________________

Match your answers against the answers given on page 121.

4

Contracting and the curriculum

Pretest

1. The first steps in **motivation management** consist of

____ a. identification of the task.
____ b. specification of the reinforcing event.
____ c. awarding of the reinforcer.
____ d. evaluation of the student's performance.

2. In contingency management, you cannot safely proceed until you specify

____ a. the size of the group.
____ b. attitude the pupil should have.
____ c. the amount of work to be completed for a specific amount of reinforcement.

3. The reinforcing event used in the educational setting can be

____ a. a purely entertaining or recreational activity.
____ b. an academic activity.
____ c. any activity which is more desirable to the student than the task activity.

4. In contingency management it is important to specify

____ a. the amount of work required.
____ b. the amount of reinforcement promised.
____ c. the beginning and termination of task and reinforcing events.

5. The appropriate tasks are determined

____ a. most accurately on an individual basis.
____ b. by the use of diagnostic tests.

6. The assignment of an **RE** (Reinforcing Event) **Area** is

a. absolutely necessary.
b. a convenient and sure way of separating task events from reinforcing events.

Match your answers against the answers given on page 122.

Summary

The Setting of the Contract Situation. The kinds of tasks the teacher may want a student to perform can range from simply "paying attention" to a demonstration, to performing workbook exercises, or presenting something in front of the class. The topics may range from arithmetic to physical education. Regardless of the subject matter, or the particular tasks to be performed, there usually will be something else which the student or students would much prefer to do. In view of this, the first steps of **motivation** management are (a) specifying the task (i.e., something the student has to do), and (b) identifying an appropriate reinforcer (i.e., something the student would rather do). It must be remembered that a reinforcing event may be any desirable change in the student's environment. The motivation manager must identify those student-desired changes which are also acceptable in the classroom situation.

Establishing the Contract. The contract must be stated in simple language, easily understood by the student. The occasion may dictate different ways of wording a particular contract, but in each case the terms of the contract will fit the paradigm, "If first you do X, then you may do (or will get) Y." The term *you,* in this paradigm, may refer to an individual student or a group of students. It is possible to reinforce the group as a whole for certain accomplishments. However, because of individual differences such as rate of progress through learning material, degree of motivation, and the kind of reward that is reinforcing in any particular situation, it is easier and more desirable to establish individual contracts with students.

This, of course, implies a need for the preparation of individual task assignments. Perhaps the easiest method is the use of programed instruction, although programed instruction is not absolutely necessary. The important thing is to establish contracts with *specifiable amounts* of work for each student, to determine their success in completing these assignments, and to reinforce their successful completion by some appropriate reward. Exactly what rewards are used depends a great deal on the teacher's observation of the student.

In general, the reinforcing event can be of two types. It can be purely *entertaining,* such as talking with the teacher, playing a game, watching a movie, etc.; or, what is most desirable from an educational point of view, it can be a preferred *academic* activity which reinforces a less preferred one. For example, it is possible to establish contracts in this manner: "First, complete the next ten arithmetic problems correctly, then you may read your *Moby Dick* for ten minutes." In this example, the teacher detected that reading *Moby Dick* was a reinforcing activity for that particular student at that particular time. If a student's preference is for arithmetic problems over reading *Moby Dick,* the contingencies would of course be reversed. The contract might then be: "Read five pages of *Moby Dick* and answer these questions; then you may work on arithmetic for ten minutes." In general, the student is the best source of information on what is reinforcing to him at any one time.

In any case, it is crucial that (a) the amount of work required and the criteria of its completion be specified, (b) the amount of reinforcement be specified, and (c) there be some clear indication of the beginning and end of tasks as well as of reinforcers.

The RE Area. One way of emphasizing the separation of the task from the reinforcement is to assign a place for task events, and another place for reinforcing events. When this is done, it is customary to refer to the area in which the reinforcements are given as a "reinforcing event area" or, more simply, the RE Area. Whether it is essential to have the RE Area geographically separated from the Task Area is not known at the present time.

Contracting in the Classroom. If there is one predictable reaction to a description of the contingency management system, it is this: "I can see how contingency contracting might work fine with individual students, but how do I handle a whole class at once?" The teacher may be asking how she can get 30 students to do the same thing at the same time and reinforce them all with the same activity. One of the main points of this section is to point out that this is not only an almost impossible task–it is unnecessary. There are three reasons for considering it almost impossible: (a) not all students need the same amount of work in the same subject area; (b) although there are exceptions to this, not all students find the same events reinforcing; (c) most important, not all students finish the assigned task at the same time. Therefore, the reinforcement could not be made contingent only upon the completion of the task; it would be contingent on two events: finishing the task and waiting for the other students to finish. This means that what would actually be reinforced would probably be sitting quietly and waiting. This is not a bad task, but it is not the task which was intended to be reinforced.

An alternative to group instruction is, of course, individual instruction. As stated before, to implement individual instruction, programed materials are convenient, though not essential, ingredients. Contingency contracting, with specified amounts of tasks and reinforcers, appears to be the ultimate achievement in the methods of individual instruction today.

It should be added that contracting with each student on an individual basis is much easier than it sounds.

Diagnosing a Student's Weaknesses. The teacher may know from personal experience what the student's weaknesses are, or he may want to determine them by means of a standardized achievement test.[1]

Once such a test has been given, the teacher should closely examine the responses the student made. The total score and relationship to national norms are not important at this point. The aim is to come up with specific parts of his behavioral repertoire which need strengthening. For example, in listing the student's weaknesses, it is useful to note that he needs work on common denominators or subtraction of fractions, rather than the generalization that he is "weak in arithmetic" or "weak in fractions."

---

[1] The California Achievement Test, available from the California Test Bureau, Del Monte Research Park, Monterey, California 93940, has been found a useful tool for this purpose.

Task Cards. Once a student's weaknesses have been determined, a plan for strengthening these areas usually suggests itself to the teacher. With this plan in mind, he can break the task to be performed into miniature tasks; these can then be written on separate cards for convenience. It is customary to refer to these cards as task cards.

For example, task cards for a particular class period may read as follows:

Card 1. Read pages 27 - 32 of your text.
Take the progress test.
If passed, take 5 minutes for reward time.
If not passed, see the teacher.

Card 2. Do the 20 problems corresponding to text pages 27 - 32.
Take the progress test.
If passed, you may read your favorite book for the rest of the period.
If not passed, see the teacher.

An RE Menu. For technical as well as practical reasons, it is convenient and efficient to have a "Reinforcing Event Menu" which lists (or pictures) a wide variety of available events that reinforce the students in the group.

The student may be allowed to choose from the menu before his task is begun or upon completion of each task. The RE menu may be updated in accordance with the student's suggestions.

Progress Checks. Progress checks are perhaps the single most important and valuable component of the contingency contracting system. First, they provide the teacher with clear indicators of the student's completion of a task assignment; if the student cannot pass the progress test, he has not yet completed his part of the contract. Second, progress checks indicate to the student when his task is finished. Third, and perhaps most important, passing a progress check leads to immediate desirable consequences. By being associated with reinforcement, the knowledge of having been correct and having successfully passed a milestone in the instructional process becomes reinforcing in itself.

A Typical School Period. A typical school period, then, might go like this. Prior to the class period, the teacher has sorted out the task cards. According to a predetermined program, each task card refers to a particular step leading toward a specific objective or goal. From previously observed contingency relationships, the teacher has also prepared a menu of reinforcing events. The student comes to the teacher, receives his task card, and chooses a reinforcing event from the menu. Such a reinforcing event may be, for example, being allowed to read a freely selected book for ten minutes. Another may be the opportunity to play a game for five minutes or perhaps the opportunity to go outside and play baseball for ten minutes. In any case, the student's receipt of his task cards, and his choice of a reinforcing event, constitute a contract.

The task cards are prepared in such a way that they indicate the beginning and termination of the task, and the criteria by which the successful termination of the task will be determined. The menus are also prepared in such a way that they specify not only the kind of reinforcing event available, but also the amount of time the student may spend on that event.

When the student successfully finishes his task by passing the progress checks, the task event is terminated and the reinforcing event is to begin. After a specified period, another signal indicates when the reinforcing time is over.

Intermediate Test

1. In arranging a contingency contract, it is necessary to specify the

____ a. number of reinforcers to be used.
____ b. amount of the task to be performed.
____ c. amount of reinforcement to be given.
____ d. beginning and termination of the reinforcing event.

2. The reinforcing event must always be

____ a. some form of entertainment.
____ b. some academic activity.
____ c. an activity desirable to the teacher.

3. On which basis is contracting usually more effective?

____ a. On a group basis.
____ b. On an individual basis.

4. Why are special RE Areas assigned?

____ a. To separate task events from reinforcing events.
____ b. Because they are absolutely necessary for a well-managed instructional situation.

5. Diagnostic tests are used in order to

____ a. determine the student's deficiencies to be remedied.
____ b. classify the student according to a standard scale.

Match your answers against the answers given on page 122.

Instructional Frames

1. A reinforcing event

____ a. must be money.
____ b. must be an activity.
____ c. may be any desirable change in the environment. c

2. The fundamental steps in contingency contracting consist of (a) specifying the task, and (b) identifying an appropriate reinforcer. Therefore, once the motivation manager has determined the necessary tasks, he must

____ a. choose what he thinks appropriate as a reward for the student's performance.
____ b. determine what changes the student desires in the environment, which are also acceptable to the teacher, and use these as reinforcers. b

3. The terms of the contract will always state what the student will receive in return for his performance. Thus, any contract will fit the paradigm:

a. "If first I do X, then you may do (or will receive) Y."
b. "If first you do X, then I may do Y."
c. "If first you do X, then you may do (or you will receive) Y." c

4. Individuals differ in such things as rate of progress through learning material and the kind of reward they are willing to work for. Because of this, it is more desirable, as well as easier, to establish contracts with

____ a. groups of students.
____ b. individual students. b

5. To establish contracts with individual students, it is necessary to prepare

____ a. group task assignments.
____ b. individual task assignments.
____ c. individual reinforcement menus. b

6. To prepare individual task assignments, it is necessary to

____ a. specify small amounts of work to be performed by each student.
____ b. specifiy reinforcers by which each student's completion of his individual task assignment may be rewarded. a

7. Any desirable change in the environment may be a reinforcing event. This means that

____ a. a reinforcing event must be something the student accepts passively, such as candy.
____ b. a reinforcing event may be a kind of academic activity which is more desirable to the student than the task is. b

8. Assume that for a particular student, the order of preference of three academic activities from most to least preferred is as follows: 1) arithmetic, 2) reading, and 3) writing. On the basis of this preference hierarchy, it should be possible for this particular student to reinforce

____ a. reading with writing.
____ b. writing with arithmetic.
____ c. arithmetic with reading.
____ d. writing with reading.
____ e. arithmetic with writing.
____ f. reading with arithmetic. b, d, f

9. Assume that a student prefers reading his assigned book, *Huckleberry Finn,* to doing arithmetic. What kind of contract would work with this student?

____ a. "First complete the next 10 arithmetic problems correctly, then you may read *Huckleberry Finn* for 10 minutes."

____ b. "Read 5 pages of *Huckleberry Finn* and answer these questions; then you may work on arithmetic for 10 minutes."

a

10. One of the rules of contracting, discussed in Chapter 3, was that the contract must be clear. This rule must apply to the performance of the contract as well. It is necessary to establish clear signals or indicators of the beginning and end of both task and reinforcement events. This means that the student should know when

____ a. his task is to begin.

____ b. he is finished with his task.

____ c. his reinforcement time is to begin.

____ d. his reinforcement ends and his next task begins.

a, b, c, d

11. For the successful use of motivation management in contracting, it is necessary to

____ a. specify the amount of work required.

____ b. specify the amount of reinforcement to be given.

____ c. establish clear signals or indicators of the beginning and end of both task and reinforcement events.

a, b, c

12. Often in classrooms using contingency contracting, a separate area is established for reinforcing events. In such cases, this special area is called the RE Area. It is clear that the establishment of such an RE Area makes it easier to

____ a. avoid wasting space.

____ b. separate the task from reinforcement events.

b

13. In order to prepare task assignments for individual students, it is necessary to know

____ a. what we want the student to learn.
____ b. what the student already knows. a and b

14. Knowing what the student is expected to learn, and what he already knows, makes it possible to

____ a. determine the student's weaknesses.
____ b. determine what the student should learn next. a and b

15. There are standardized tests that are designed to determine the student's level of knowledge in various areas. Examining an individual student's scores on such a test in detail will make it possible to

____ a. determine his weaknesses.
____ b. determine what might be needed to remedy these weaknesses. a and b

16. In using achievement tests as diagnostic tests, it would be important to note, for example, that

____ a. the student "doesn't know how to recognize nouns and verbs."
____ b. the student is "weak in English." a

17. Once the student's weaknesses are determined, the next step is to

____ a. label the student as high, average, or below average.
____ b. determine what instruction and materials will be necessary for the student to remedy his deficiencies. b

18. With a plan in mind to remedy a student's weaknesses, the teacher can

____ a. send the student to remedial classes.
____ b. break the total remedial task into miniature tasks. b

19. Miniature tasks may be specified on small index cards for convenience. Such a task card may read:

____ a. "Read pages 2-29 of your text. Take the progress test. If passed, take 5 minutes for reward time. If not passed, see your teacher."
____ b. "Read the first 200 pages of your text. Take the progress test. If passed, take 5 minutes for reward time. If not passed, see the teacher."
____ c. "Read pages 2-29 of your text. Then take 5 minutes for reward time."
____ d. "Read pages 2-29 of your text. Take the progress test. Then take 5 minutes of reward time." a

20. To prepare individual task assignments, it is convenient to write miniature tasks on __________ __________. task cards

21. To make it easier for the student to choose a reinforcing event, it is convenient to list a number of events that students usually find reinforcing. Such a list, which may be accompanied by pictures, is usually referred to as a reinforcing event (or RE) menu. The RE Menu is

____ a. a convenient list of reinforcing events the student may choose from.
____ b. a list of all the things that the student might find reinforcing. a

22. The best source for RE Menu items is the students themselves. Based on the students' suggestions, RE Menus may be expanded or revised. Thus, RE Menus are

____ a. lists of things the teacher wants to offer the student.
____ b. lists of things the student himself is likely to want as reinforcers. b

Post-test

1. Which of the following is correct?

____ a. It is easier to establish group contracts than it is to establish individual contracts.
____ b. Working with individual contracts is both easier and more efficient than working with group contracts.

2. Menus, as discussed in this section, are lists of

____ a. tasks (task cards).
____ b. possible reinforcing events.

3. It is important that the beginning and termination points be specified for

____ a. task events.
____ b. reinforcing events.

4. Reinforcement follows the performance of a task

____ a. regardless of its quality, if the student spent enough time on it.
____ b. only if it was performed to some specified criterion.

5. During a typical school period, the teacher will present the student with a (a)____________card. When the student receives this, he also chooses an item from the (b) ____________. Thus, a (c)______________ is made.

6. A (a) ___________ card indicates the assignment to be performed, the (b) ______________of each task event, and the (c)_______________ whereby successful completion of the task is determined.

Match your answers against the answers given on page 122.

5

Shifting to self-contracting

Pretest

1. Self-contracting is

____ a. a form of contingency contracting.
____ b. a form of self-management which can be taught to students.

2. Positive contingency contracts may be

____ a. manager controlled.
____ b. student controlled.
____ c. transitional.

3. Contracts in which the task events that are required and the reinforcing events offered are determined by a manager are called ____________________-controlled contracts.

4. In student-controlled contracts, the amount of tasks and the amount of reinforcement are determined by the ______________.

5. The aim of the contingency contract system is to lead the student from (a) ________________-controlled contracting to (b) ________________-controlled contracting.

6. In transitional contracting, the contingencies and amounts are determined by

____ a. the manager alone.
____ b. the student alone.
____ c. both the manager and the student.

7. The only major differences between micro-contracts and macro-contracts is that in macro-contracts the task events are always ________________________________.

Match your answers against the answers given on page 123.

Summary

Every conscientious teacher wants to do more than teach arithmetic, composition, geography, or whatever his subject matter is. He would also like to help students develop such attributes as self-control, initiative, and self-discipline.

Everyone agrees that these characteristics are important. The trouble is that there are no academic courses that equip an instructor to teach the behavior characteristics that these terms describe or label. Contingency contracting in which the student is his own contractor—a process we are calling **self-contracting**—offers promise of a concrete way to begin teaching self-management. Since so little is known about the teaching of self-management, it offers a great opportunity for the experimentally minded teacher to try out various techniques of his own.

There are some important constraints to be noticed in pioneering efforts[1] at teaching self-contracting. In the first place, some agent other than the student determines both the task requirement and the length of reinforcement time. The difficulties to be encountered in bringing a student eventually to the point where he determines both of these factors for himself are, at present, not well known. In what follows, we will

---

[1]Approximations to self-contracting are presently in use by McKee in a prison (Clark, 1966), and in a Job Corps Center by Westinghouse Learning Corp. (Chadwick, 1967). In the Job Corps Center, at the beginning of a typical class period the student goes to a previously designated task card file, removes a task card, follows it with a reinforcing event card, then selects another task card, and so on, until he has his day's contract. The RE card permits the student to roll two dice which determine the length of time his reinforcement will be. (Reinforcing time is twice the value in minutes of the number the student rolls; if he rolls a seven, for example, he gets fourteen minutes in the RE area.) Though the student is given all of his contracts for a whole school period, he is advised to take his RE time after the completion of *each* contract. (Dr. John N. McKee, Rehabilitation Research Foundation, Elmore, Ala.)

present an analysis of the ways in which the contingency contracting system may lead to successive approximations to self-management through the possibilities available in the system.

Types of Contingency Contracting. Positive contingency contracts may be of three basic types, depending on whether the terms of the contract are determined by a **manager,** the **student** himself, or, in a number of **transitional** possibilities, by both of these.

So far, we have discussed the forms of contracting which are involved in *manager-controlled* contracts. In these contracts, the amounts of the task event required and the reinforcing event offered are determined by a manager, who may be a parent, a teacher, or someone else in a position to deliver rewards for accomplishment. This kind of contracting is very different from what might be called the *student-controlled* contract.

In student-controlled contracts, both the amount of task and the amount of reinforcement are determined by the student himself. The aim of the contingency contracting system is this: to lead the student from the manager-controlled contracting method to the student-controlled contracting method. This may be accomplished by a transition through five levels, which might be called *transitional* contracting.

In the following analysis of the three types of contracting, it will be assumed that the rules specified in Chapter 3 of this book are followed. In addition, it is assumed that the amount of the reinforcing event is determined and made known to the student *prior to* the establishment of the amount of the required task event.

Level One: Manager-Controlled Contracting

In the *manager-controlled* contracting system, the procedural steps are as follows:

Step 1. The manager determines the amount of reinforcement to be given.

Step 2. The manager determines the amount of task to be required.

Step 3. The manager presents this contract to the student.

Step 4. The student accepts the contract and performs the task.

Step 5. The manager delivers the reward.

In the *student-controlled* contracting situation, the procedure is similar to the one described above. The difference is that the student replaces the manager. The student himself determines the amount of the reinforcement and the amount of the task, agrees to his own contract, performs the task, and delivers the reinforcement to himself. In *transitional* contracts, both the manager and the student are involved in determining the terms of the contract.

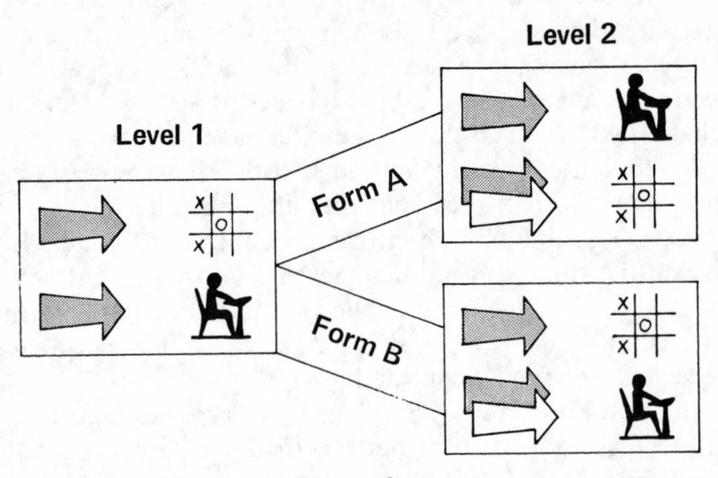

Figure 1

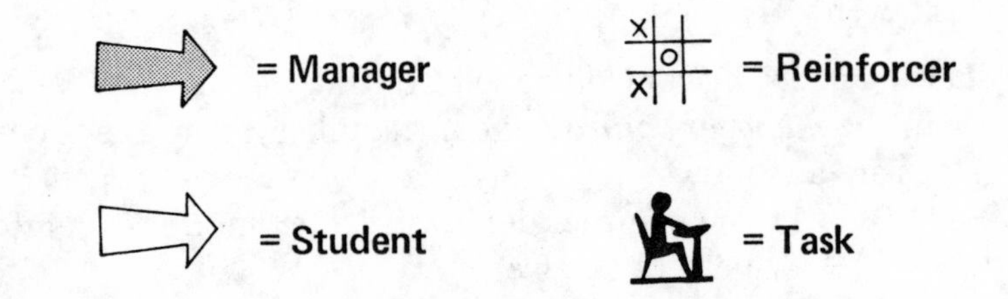

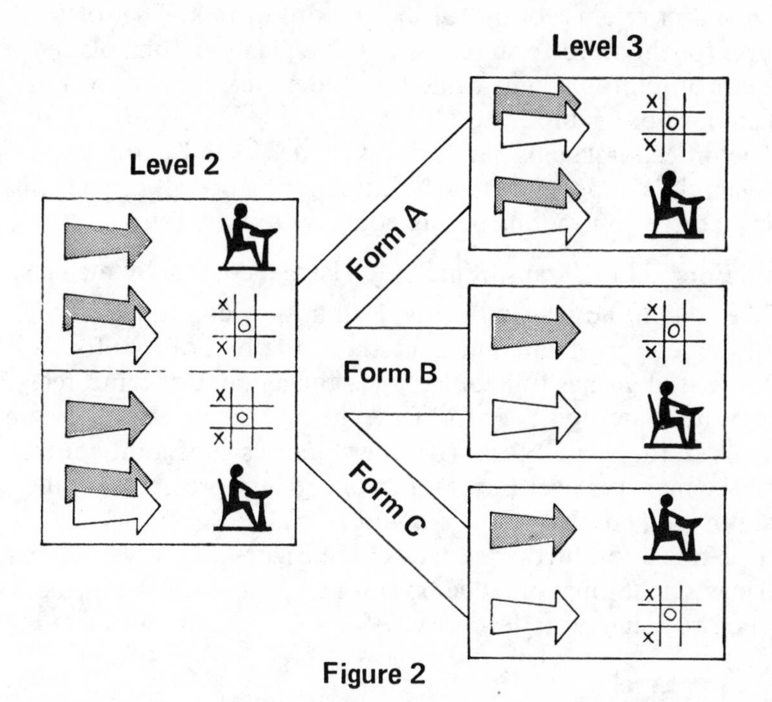

Figure 2

Level Two: First Transitional Step–Partial control by student

The first transitional step follows manager-controlled contracts. Either (A) the student assumes joint control with the manager over the amount of reinforcement to be given, while the manager retains full control of the amount of task; or (B) the student assumes joint control with the manager over the amount of task, while the manager retains full control of the amount of reinforcement. Whichever of the two forms (A or B) follows level one, the other form must also be practiced before going on to level three.

The first-level procedural steps, therefore, expand outward as in Figure 1.

Level Three: Second Transitional Step–Equal control by manager and student

The next transitional step requires three forms of contracting. In one of these (A), the student and the manager share joint determination of both the amount of reinforcement and the amount of task. In the second form (B), the student assumes responsibility for the amount of reinforcement, while the manager retains control of the amount of task. The roles reverse for the third form (C), where the manager controls the amount of reinforcement while the student assumes control of the amount of his task.

The procedural steps have now expanded as in Figure 2.

Again, it is important that the student practice all three forms of level three contracting before going on to level four.

Level Four: Third Transitional Step—Partial control by manager

The student now becomes involved in the determination of both the reinforcement and the task. In the first of two forms (A), the student has full control over the amount of reinforcement, and shares joint control with the manager over the amount of task. In the second form (B), the student shares joint control with the manager over the amount of the reinforcement, while assuming full control of the amount of task.

This transition further expands as in Figure 3.

The student must practice both forms of level four contracting before going on to level five.

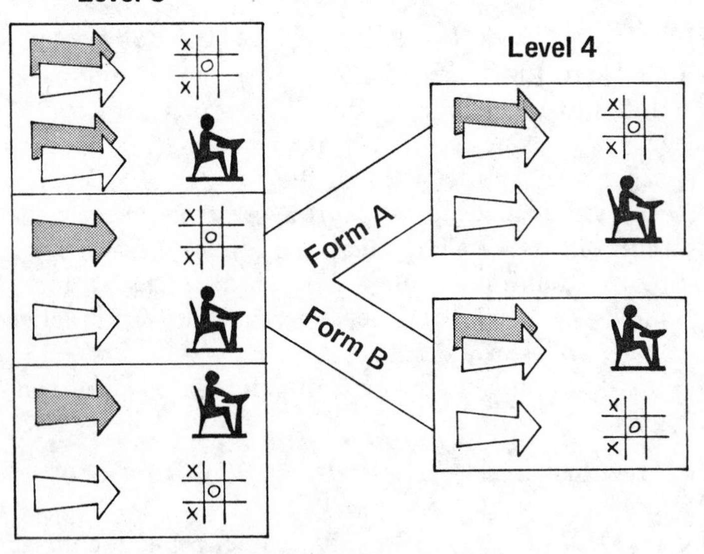

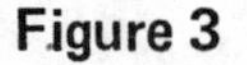
Figure 3

Level Five: Student-Controlled Contracting

From the completion of level four, it is a natural consequence that the student take over complete control.

Implementation of the Transition. In order to speed the student's arrival at the final stage of self-management, the making and fulfilling of contracts may be considered as major or *macro-tasks* in larger *macro-contracts* which are prepared specifically to reward contracting as a behavior. The macro-contract in such a case might say: "If you make and complete twenty small contracts, you will earn a ticket to the movies." The small contracts constituting tasks under macro-contracts may then be called *micro-contracts.* In this sense, the first four chapters of this book deal with the types and uses of micro-contracts. It is obvious, however, that to the extent that the student is involved in making, or at least accepting and fulfilling such micro-contracts, he is performing tasks. It then follows that these contracting-tasks can also be contracted according to the principles of contingency contracting. Therefore, what has been said so far about contracting will generally hold true equally well for both micro-contracts and macro-contracts, the only difference being that in macro-contracts the task events are *always* micro-contracts.

It is possible that some students, after only a few illustrative examples, will be able to start making micro-contracts at levels higher than level 1. Some of them may even be able to

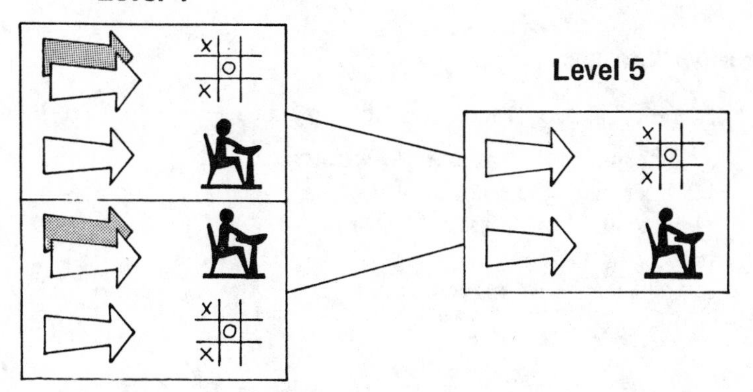

Figure 4

make self-controlled (level 5) contracts. The making of such micro-contracts should, therefore, be reinforced according to the principles of contracting defined in this book.

In this chapter we have stressed that if the student's motivation is to continue progressing under conditions outside of the relationship established between himself and the contingency manager, it seems necessary for him to learn how to establish himself as his own contingency manager. Shifting from management-by-contracts to self-management must also be followed with these macro-contracts. Control of the specification of the macro-tasks will eventually be shifted from manager-control to student-control, and the student will have to be able to reinforce himself under such macro-contracts.

The ultimate goal of contingency contracting can now be redefined as *getting the student ready to both establish and fulfill his own contracts, and to reinforce himself, under macro-contracts, for doing so.* Having had such practice in self-determination, the student becomes ready to take over full control and determine for himself the amounts of both reinforcements and tasks. Through these transitional procedures, we arrive at a point where the student is capable of making his own contracts, determining his own tasks, and determining his own reinforcements. At this stage, it is expected that the individual can maintain motivational independence by using contingency management as a procedure for systematic self-management.

Intermediate Test

1. In a manager-controlled contract, the manager

____ a. determines the amount of reinforcing event.
____ b. determines the amount of task.
____ c. presents the contract to the student.
____ d. accepts the contract and performs the task.
____ e. delivers the payoff reward.

2. In student-controlled contracts, the student

____ a. determines the amount of reinforcement.
____ b. determines the amount of task.
____ c. agrees to assume the contract.
____ d. performs the task.
____ e. delivers the reinforcement to himself.

3. The difference between the level two contract and the manager-controlled contract is that

____ a. the manager and the student determine the amount of the reinforcement, and the manager determines the task.
____ b. the manager determines the amount of the reinforcement, and the manager and the student jointly determine the amount of the task.
____ c. either of the above.

4. In the second transitional step (level three), the student may determine

____ a. the reinforcement if the task is determined by the manager.
____ b. the task if the reinforcement is determined by the manager.
____ c. both the reinforcement and the task jointly with the manager.

5. In the third transitional step (level four), the manager has

____ a. joint control with the student over both the task and the reinforcing event.
____ b. full control over the reinforcing event only.
____ c. full control over the task and no control over the reinforcing event.
____ d. joint control over first one of the two events, then over the other.

6. Macro-contracts are contracts in which the task is the fulfillment of ______________________.

7. The ultimate goal of contingency contracting is

a. getting the student ready to establish and fulfill his own contracts so that he may be reinforced for doing so by a manager using macro-contracts.

b. getting the student ready to establish and fulfill both his own micro-contracts and his own macro-contracts.

Match your answers against the answers given on page 123.

Instructional Frames

1. A form of contingency contracting in which the student is his own contractor may be called

____ a. self-contracting.
____ b. student-controlled contracting. a and b

2. The situation that has been dealt with in previous chapters of this book may be described as

____ a. student-controlled contracting.
____ b. manager-controlled contracting. b

3. In manager-controlled contracting, the amount of task and the amount of reinforcement are determined by

____ a. the student himself.
____ b. a contingency manager (e.g., teacher or parent). b

4. Self-management is the ultimate goal of the contingency management system. Leading the student from management-by-others to self-management is equivalent to

____ a. shifting from manager-controlled contracts to student-controlled contracts.
____ b. shifting from student-controlled contracts to manager-controlled contracts. a

5. Between manager-controlled contracts and student-controlled contracts there are a number of transitional possibilities. These transitional states should give gradually increasing control over the contracts to the

____ a. manager.
____ b. student. b

6. Five major events take place in all forms of positive contracting. These are:
   1. determination of the amount of reinforcement,
   2. determination of the amount of task,
   3. presentation of the contract,
   4. acceptance and performance of the contract, and
   5. delivery of the payoff.

   In a manager-controlled contract, 1, 2, 3, and 5 above are performed by the (a)_______________ and 4 is performed by the (b)_______________.

   a. manager
   b. student

7. In student-controlled contracting (level five), which numbers of the five events listed in frame 6 are performed by the manager? _______________

   none

8. As may be expected, transitional contracts, which are to lead the student from manager-controlled to student-controlled contracting situations, are such that

   ____ a. all five events of a contracting situation are performed by the manager.
   ____ b. all five events are performed by the student.
   ____ c. some of the five events are performed by the manager and others are performed by the student.

   c

9. It is readily seen that, of the five events, events 1 and 2 are the most critical. These are the major events that are influenced by transitional contracting. Transitional contracts, then, are contracts in which the student takes a greater and greater role in

   ____ a. determining the amount of reinforcement.
   ____ b. determining the amount of task.

   a and b

10. In the first transitional step (level two), the student shares a portion of the responsibility of determining the contracts. This means that

___ a. the student may determine the amount of the reinforcement by himself.

___ b. the manager and the student together may determine the amount of the reinforcement, but the manager would determine the amount of the task.

___ c. the manager would determine the amount of reinforcement, and the manager and the student may jointly determine the amount of the task.

___ d. b and c in turn.

d

11. In the first transitional step we may have

___ a. joint determination of the reinforcement and manager determination of the task.

___ b. manager determination of the reinforcement and joint determination of the task.

a and b in turn

12. Partial control is given to the student in the ______________ transitional step.

first

13. The first transitional step consists of giving (a)______________ control to the student. This is done first by allowing the student to participate in determining either the amount of (b)__________ or the amount of (c)______________.

a. partial
b. task
c. reinforcement

14. In the second transitional step (level three), the student and the manager share equal responsibility in determining the terms of the contract. This may be done by

___ a. the manager determining the reinforcement and the student determining the task.
___ b. the student determining the reinforcement and the manager determining the task.
___ c. the manager and the student jointly determining both the amount of the reinforcement and the amount of the task.
___ d. all of these three alternatives, in turn.

d

15. In the second transitional step, the student and the manager have ________________ control over the terms of the contract.

equal

16. In the second transitional step there are

a. two alternatives.
b. three alternatives.
c. four alternatives.

b

17. The alternatives in the second transitional step are:

a. ____

____

b. ____

____

c. ____

____

a. manager controls the task, student controls the reinforcement.
b. student controls the task, manager controls the reinforcement.
c. joint control of both the task and reinforcement.

18. In the third or last transitional step (level four), the manager's role is greatly reduced. The student is involved in the determination of both the task and the reinforcement. However, he shares one of these with the manager. Thus, in the last transitional step, the (a) __________ is involved in the determination of both the task and the reinforcement, and the (b) __________ participates in the determination of either the task or the reinforcing event, but not both.

a. student
b. manager

19. Counting manager-controlled and student-controlled contracts, and the three transitional steps, we have __________ levels of contracting, each leading to an increasingly greater level of self-management by the student.

five

20. In level one (manager-controlled contracting), both the task and the reinforcement are determined by the __________ alone.

manager

21. In level two, which is the (a) __________ transitional step, the (b) __________ is involved in the determination of both the task and the reinforcement. The (c) __________ is involved in only one of these.

a. first
b. manager
c. student

22. Level three is the (a) __________ transitional step. At this level, there is (b) __________ participation by the student and the manager in the determination of the contract.

a. second
b. equal

23. Equal participation by manager and student can be shared in __________ different ways.

three

24. Level four is transitional step number (a) __________. At this level, the (b) __________ is involved in the determination of both the task and the reinforcement. The (c) __________ is involved in only one of these.

a. three
b. student
c. manager

25. Level five is the goal of contingency management. This is called ________________-controlled contracting. At this level,

____ a. there is partial determination of task and reinforcement by the student.
____ b. full determination of task and reinforcement by the student.
____ c. full determination of task and reinforcement by the manager.
____ d. partial determination of task and reinforcement by the manager.

student
b

26. The idea of contingency contracting is to reward the student for his performance. If we want to teach the student to prepare his own contracts and perform under these contracts, the way to motivate him is to

____ a. use threat of punishment.
____ b. use contingency contracting.

b

27. A contract in which the task itself is to prepare and complete a small contract may be called a

____ a. macro-task.
____ b. macro-contract.
____ c. micro-task.
____ d. micro-contract.

b

28. The same rules would apply to macro-contracts as those that apply to micro-contracts. The difference is that in macro-contracts the tasks would always be

____ a. determined by the student.
____ b. micro-contracts.

b

29. Under macro-contracts, the student may be rewarded for performing under

____ a. manager-controlled contracting.
____ b. transitional contracting.
____ c. student-controlled contracting.

a, b, c

30. Macro-contracts themselves may be

____ a. manager-controlled.
____ b. transitional.
____ c. student-controlled.

a, b, c

31. The ultimate goal of contingency contracting is to help the student to become his own contingency manager. This means that the student should be helped to eventually

____ a. perform under self-controlled micro-contracts.
____ b. perform under manager-controlled micro-contracts.
____ c. perform under self-controlled macro-contracts, whose tasks are self-controlled micro-contracts.
____ d. perform under manager-controlled macro-contracts whose tasks are self-controlled micro-contracts.

c

32. Self-management, by the definition used in this analysis, consists of the student performing under self-controlled (a) ____________-contracts, when the individual tasks are self-controlled (b) ____________-contracts.

a. macro-contracts
b. micro-contracts

Post-test

1. Describe the five levels of contingency contracting, each of which leads to increasingly greater levels of self-management.

1. ____
____
2. ____
____
3. ____
____
4. ____
____
5. ____
____

2. "If you make and complete twenty small contracts, you will earn a ticket to the movies." This is an exampie of a ____________________- contract.

Match your answers against the answers given on page 123.

6

A note about resistance and opposition

Contingency management is difficult to teach some people. No one is sure of the reason for this. We will examine a number of possible reasons for this difficulty; the reader is asked to judge for himself whether any of these reasons are relevant to his own reactions to the system.

Contingency Management Concepts Are Too Simple. In a limited sense at least, those who will use this program already know about the effects of reward and punishment. As a matter of fact, those to whom contingency management is difficult to teach will often insist they know all about these classes of events. (It sometimes seems as though the only ones who do not understand these events perfectly are the psychologists who have been studying them for the last fifty years.) As a matter of fact, the concepts involved in contingency management *are* simple. There must be some other source of difficulty.

Is It Inertia? It is often said of educators that they are reluctant to change their ways of doing things. This widespread concept of an educator as one who resists innovation is exemplified by the following quotation from a weekly magazine: "In many American schools, . . . the prevailing attitudes are inflexibility, defensiveness and insularity. . ." (*Time,* January 20, 1967, p. 18)

However, it has been our experience that most teachers are not only willing but eager to try out methods which promise greater control over the behavior of their students.

Is Contingency Management Bribery? The term bribery has strong connotations of immorality. A bribe is used to induce someone to commit an act which is, in some way, illegal or unethical. None of these characteristics is true for the kinds of behavior we are discussing in this program. But there is more to it than that. Many people (particularly parents) somehow resent having to arrange payoffs for the child's behavior. "The child is supposed to behave because I tell him to, not because I am holding out a reward for him," is a common reaction.

This attitude probably arises out of the traditions of our society. There is no instant remedy, but it may help to point out that all of us—children and adults alike—do what we do because of the anticipated (sometimes long-range) consequences of what we do.

The Automatic Nature of Reinforcement. The effects of contingency relationships must be assumed to function at all times, independently of whether they are understood, approved of, hated or loved. People sometimes mistakenly say, for example, "A reinforcement won't work with this subject because he is too young (or mentally retarded or obtuse) to understand why he is being rewarded." This argument does not hold up when one considers that in nature's scheme of things, animals as lowly as insects and worms react to reward and punishment contingencies; and, on the other end of the scale, the extent to which our own adult actions are guided by their real or expected consequences.

In summary, contingencies, whether they are systematically arranged or occur by chance or inadvertence, whether approved or disapproved, understood or not, will have their effect. Always.

Criterion Test for Part I

1. In a positive contingency contract,

____ a. the terms may imply avoidance of punishment.
____ b. a reward is offered, dependent upon the successful completion of a specified task.

2. "Last year there were 465 traffic violations in the city of Putumayo." The violators broke ______________ contracts.

3. Two criteria for an effective reward are:

a. ______________________________
b. ______________________________

4. An event, when it follows a particular act of behavior, which increases the likelihood that the act will be repeated, is technically known as a ______________.

5. List the ten rules of contingency contracting. Contracting must be:

a. ______________
b. ______________
c. ______________
d. ______________
e. ______________

The contract should reward:
f. ______________
g. ______________
h. ______________
i. ______________
j. ______________

6. To maintain an unwanted behavior, it is best to (a)______________ its occurrence. To eliminate it, it must not (b) ______________.

7. Describe a typical school period under contingency management.

8. In applying contingency management in a classroom situation, it is important that the contract specify three things. These are:

a. ______________________________

b. ______________________________

c. ______________________________

9. A reinforcing event in a classroom

____ a. must be some form of entertainment.

____ b. may be an academic activity.

____ c. may be anything that is more desirable to the student than the task activity.

10. What is a macro-contract?

11. What is a micro-contract?

12. What is a transitional contract?

13. Should a macro-contract be a negative contract?

14. Could a task event become a reinforcing event?

15. Describe the five levels of contracting, leading to self-management.

Level 1. ______________________________

____

Level 2. ______________________________

____

Level 3. ______________________________

____

Level 4. ______________________________

____

Level 5. ______________________________

____

Match your answers against the answers given on pages 124 and 125.

PART II

APPLYING CONTINGENCY CONTRACTING IN THE CLASSROOM

INTRODUCTION

The second part of this book is designed to teach the application of contingency contracting procedures in the typical instructional setting. It assumes the reader has learned the principles and rules of contingency contracting as described in the first part of the book.

This second part, in addition to expanding on the procedures described in the preceding chapters, also contains suggestions for analyzing the course curriculum to make possible selection of self-instructional materials essential to the system. These suggestions are based on the assumption that the reader has had previous instruction or experience in curriculum design and test construction.

Flowcharts and illustrations are also provided. The tables are to serve as illustrative examples and tools of analysis for the teacher. The flowcharts are intended as instructional guides for those who have already successfully completed the material. They are referenced to specific portions of the text for quick access.

At the end of each chapter you will find a Post-test, as in Part I. The authors recommend that you try your hand at each of these before you begin reading that chapter, so that it functions as a Pretest. Then when you have completed the material contained in that chapter, you can test your mastery of its content in the usual way.

7

Preparation of materials

Preparing Task Materials

When you prepare the required task materials for the contingency managed classroom you must accomplish the following four steps:

- Identify and describe the subject areas.
- Break down the subject area objectives into daily task units.
- Collect materials for subject areas.
- Divide materials into task units.

The following sections describe each of these steps in greater detail.

Identify and Describe the Subject Areas. This book assumes the reader has some training or experience in methods and material preparation for elementary or high school teaching. Any teacher must obviously have some idea what he is teaching and why he wants his students to learn it—although some teachers may be able to describe this more coherently and in greater detail than others. It is relatively easy for the high school teacher to identify and describe the curriculum or any part of it. In high school, the teacher usually deals basically with only one subject area, such as social studies, English, algebra, etc. The elementary teacher, who deals with a wider range of subjects, may have trouble focusing on a specific description of one part of the curriculum.

While this book cannot cover the entire subject of curricular planning, we must emphasize the importance of describing educational subject matter in terms of the behaviors the student will be capable of when the educational activity is completed. If a description of an educational objective is fuzzy, such as "The student must understand sentence structure," the instructional process based on that goal is likely to fail. Instead, educational objectives should be stated in terms of observable student behavior. Some examples are: "The student must correctly select simple and complex sentences and sentence fragments from an assortment." "The student must use capital letters correctly in the initial words of sentences."

A brief, authoritative, and easy-to-understand book on this subject is *Preparing Instructional Objectives,* by Robert Mager (Sear Publishers, 1963). It is worthwhile reading for any teacher, and particularly for one who intends to apply contingency management.

When you specify the subject areas of a contingency management system in terms of behavioral objectives, there are two significant consequences:

- You will be able to observe the student's progress and be assured that he is satisfactorily acquiring the knowledge and skills you have specified.
- You can identify and/or prepare diagnostic test items which can be scored and correlated with specific instructional materials.

Break Down the Subject into Daily Task Units. Daily tasks are roughly equivalent to the daily lesson plans prepared by the teacher. They should be the basis for day-by-day individual task assignments for each student. The daily tasks will assure a logical and consistent flow of the instructional sequence from one unit to the next. It is important that task units be as short as possible so the student can complete them and receive the contracted reinforcement. In the typical 50-minute high school period the average student should successfully complete at least two task assignments and the same number of reinforcing event periods.

Collect Materials for Subject Areas. Once the subject area is identified as, for example, mathematics, reading, history, science, the next step is to determine what subject materials exist to cover this area. These materials may be programed courses, audio-visual materials, workbooks, textbooks, ordinary library books, or oral communications. What is important is that materials should be evaluated to indicate high correlation between the objectives for the student in the subject matter being taught and the content of the instructional materials. In addition, it would be helpful to have materials geared to several different student levels within the same general subject area. For example, if the subject area is seventh grade reading, the teacher could have materials appropriate for students reading on fifth, sixth, seventh, and eighth grade levels. At first it may be impossible for the teacher to get materials other than those specified by the state board, but if additional materials are needed, they can probably be requisitioned at specified times during the year. In some cases they can be borrowed from other teachers, or improvised.

Divide Materials into Daily Tasks. Once materials have been collected for a particular subject area, they should be analyzed and assigned to correspond to the daily task objectives. You may prefer to do this before the school year begins, or prior to introducing any new unit of instruction, or on a day-by-day basis. If you choose to assign materials for task objectives before school begins, you would choose materials corresponding to the subject, divide the materials by chapters, etc., corresponding to units within the subject, and finally assign specific pages as tasks within the unit.

Instructional Frames

1. The best way to describe a behavioral objective is a statement of

____ a. how much subject matter the teacher will present.

____ b. how much time the teacher will spend on the subject.

____ c. whether the student will know and understand the subject.

____ d. what the student will be able to do when the teaching has been completed. d

2. Which of the following is a good example of a behavioral objective?

____ a. The student should appreciate good music.
____ b. The student should be able to solve any multiplication problem with a two-place multiplier.
____ c. The student should know multiplication.
____ d. The student should know how to read. — b

3. The first step in preparing materials for a contingency management program is to identify and describe the s________________ matter in terms of b______________________ o_______________________. — subject, behavioral objectives

4. After the subject matter has been identified and described, the subject matter should be subdivided into

____ a. units small enough to be presented in daily lessons.
____ b. units small enough for a school marking period. — a

5. The best short rule to cover the length of task units is

____ a. they should be long enough to fill the allotted time.
____ b. they should follow the chapter or lesson divisions in textbooks.
____ c. the shorter, the better. — c

6. The most important thing to consider in selecting materials for a subject area is that the materials match the

____ a. generally accepted curriculum for the grade level.
____ b. most logical organization of the content.
____ c. behavioral objectives for the course. — c

7. Ideally, the level of difficulty of the materials should be matched to

___ a. the average student in your class.
___ b. several different levels of ability.
___ c. the lowest level of ability in your class.

b

8. The first three steps in the process of preparing materials are

a. ________________ and ________________ the subject areas.
b. Break down the subject area objectives into __________ __________ units.
c. Collect ______________________ for the subject areas.

a. Identify describe
b. daily task
c. materials

9. Materials should be divided into daily task units in such a way that they match the organization of the

___ a. task units developed by the teacher for the subject matter.
___ b. traditional sequence of teaching the subject matter.
___ c. textbooks being used.

a

10. List the four steps in preparing materials:

a. Identify and ______________ the ____________ ______________.
b. Break down the ______________ ____________ into __________ __________ ___________.
c. __________ ________________ for the subject areas.
d. __________ the ________________ into __________ __________ __________.

a. describe, subject matter
b. subject matter, daily task units
c. Collect materials
d. Divide materials, daily task units

Preparation of Diagnostic Test Materials

Diagnostic test materials fulfill two purposes. First, they are the only way a student's strengths and weaknesses can be determined objectively. Second, use of diagnostic-type test items can assure the teacher that a student has completed a particular task assignment and thus fulfilled his contingency contract.

Diagnostic tests which fill the first of these functions are used for preparing prescriptions for the correction of specific weaknesses, and are called **prescriptive tests.** They should be given before any new unit of instruction is introduced. The second type of test, called a **progress check**, is designed to determine if the student has learned the information contained in a specific amount of reading material, in a lecture, a film, or other type of presentation. If he can pass the progress check, he receives his reward; if not, remedial action must be taken to make sure that he can pass.

The major difference between progress checks and prescriptive tests is that progress check items cover more minute details of the instructional subject. Diagnostic test materials must be obtained either by identification of existing diagnostic test materials or by preparation of diagnostic test items where none exist.

Identifying Existing Diagnostic Test Materials. In some subject areas, diagnostic test materials of prescriptive value can be found in standardized form. Examples are the Stanford Achievement Test, the California Achievement Test, and other similar tests.[1] Items on these tests are generally made to correspond to a specific level of instruction in several areas. For example, in the California Achievement Test, several levels may be identified for third grade reading. Such tests can be used then for placing the student at a particular achievement level and prescribing tasks appropriate to the next achievement range for which specific items exist on the test. In addition to these standardized tests, self-instructional materials often contain

---

[1]Some fine tests (some still in the developmental stages) may be obtained from the Learning Research and Development Center, Univ. of Pittsburgh, or Research for Better Schools, Philadelphia, Pa.

valuable diagnostic test items. Most of these are the progress check type, which examine in detail the repertoire of the student regarding specific items in the material. If the teacher has already correlated materials with the instructional objectives, these tests will serve directly as progress checks for the specified tasks.

Preparation of Diagnostic Test Items. In areas where diagnostic test materials do not exist, or where it is not feasible to administer and grade standardized tests, the teacher will have to prepare diagnostic test items for prescriptive tests, for progress checks, or both. For prescriptive purposes, items should be prepared to cover the tasks specified for the entire year, and test items should be developed based on the materials assigned to each unit of instruction. The teacher could make up the final examination and administer it as a prescriptive test early in the school year.

Progress checks should be based on the daily task materials. For each item of the daily task list the teacher should prepare from two to five objective questions for progress checks. Ideally, progress checks should be written so students can grade their own or exchange papers with one another. In addition, unit tests should be administered to determine if the student has mastered the material and is ready to progress to a new level. If the student had been cheating, it is unlikely that he would pass a unit test. The unit test could contain sample test items taken from several progress checks over the material covered. It could be administered as part of the prescriptive test, in which case the test would contain review items as well as items on materials to be covered in the next unit. If the reader has not had experience in constructing test items, he might refer to Dorothy Adkins Wood's book *Test Construction.* [2]

Correlation of Task Materials and Test Materials.

Once test items have been matched to the instructional materials specified, it is easy to correlate scores on these diagnostic

---

[2] Wood, Dorothy Adkins. *Test Construction: Development and Interpretation of Achievement Tests.* Charles E. Merrill Books, Inc., Columbus, Ohio, 1961.

tests with specific portions of the instructional materials. Portions of the California Achievement Test, for example, may be assigned to specified units of instruction. A given student, having taken a diagnostic test for prescriptive purposes, may pass the items corresponding to the first unit objectives, but fail the second and later ones. Thus the materials corresponding to the second and later objectives would be his task assignments. Then, as he completes each of the daily task assignments for the appropriate unit, the student takes the progress check corresponding to the completed task.

Instructional Frames

1. Diagnostic test materials are useful to a teacher both before and ____________ the task assignment. — after

2. A prescriptive test is one that is used to

____ a. prepare an individual prescription for instruction.
____ b. determine what grade a student should receive.
____ c. determine whether a unit of instruction was successful. — a

3. A progress check is normally given

____ a. before a unit of instruction is assigned.
____ b. after a unit of instruction is assigned. — b

4. The two types of diagnostic tests are called

____________________ ________
________________ __________ — prescriptive test; progress check

5. The most detailed types of questions are usually used in

____ a. tests given to diagnose or prescribe a student's weaknesses.
____ b. tests given to measure what a student learned during a unit of instruction. — b

Flowchart No. 1
Task, Material, and Diagnostic Test Specification
(See Chapter 7)

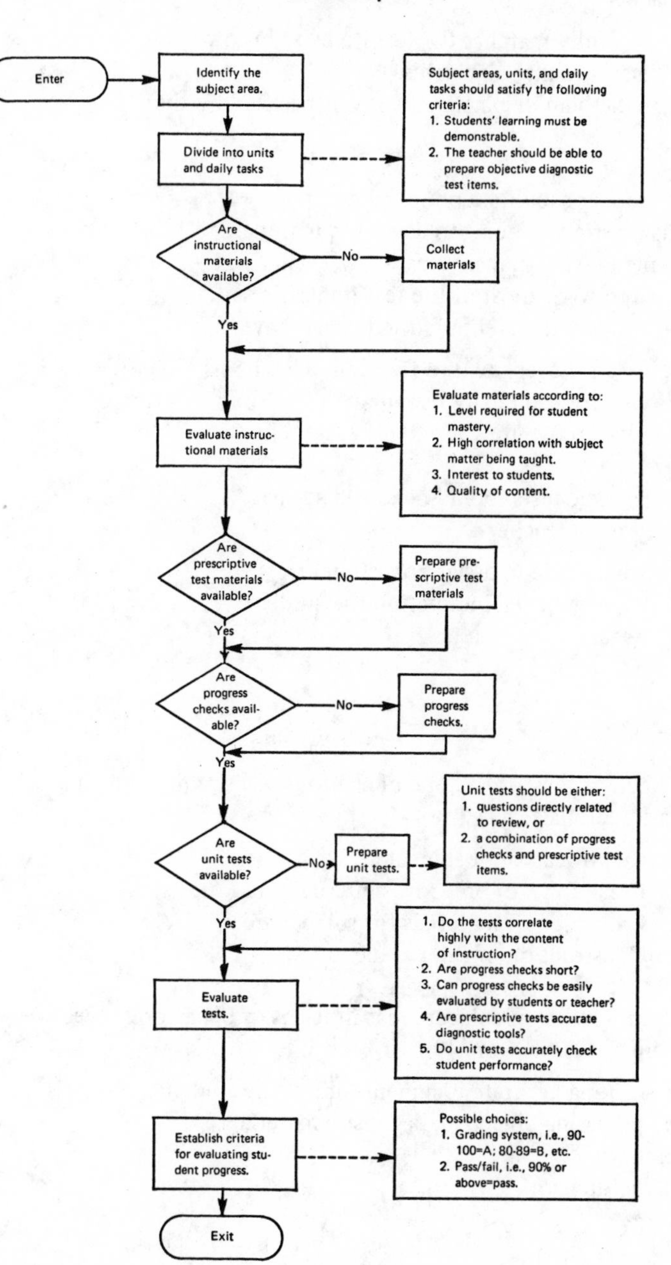

6. Existing printed materials, such as published tests and programmed texts, can be used as sources of diagnostic tests by a teacher, provided that the teacher

____ a. carefully matches the test items to his own instructional objectives.
____ b. uses them in exactly the form specified by the publisher.

a

7. A teacher should be prepared with ample diagnostic test items to cover the material being taught. In many cases the teacher will have to write most of the test items himself. How many items should the teacher have?

____ a. One for every two to five daily task items
____ b. One for each daily task item
____ c. Two to five for every daily task item

c

8. Diagnostic tests should be keyed so that they tell a teacher

____ a. what grade to assign to a student.
____ b. what remedial instruction the student needs.

b

Post-test

1. Which of these is *not* one of the four steps required for preparing task materials?

____ a. Identification of subject areas
____ b. Breakdown of objectives into daily task units
____ c. Collection of materials for subject areas
____ d. Construction of the RE menu

2. Specification of subject areas in terms of behavioral objectives will help the teacher in

____ a. making accurate judgments about the students' progress.
____ b. preparing objective diagnostic materials.
____ c. both.
____ d. neither.

3. Division of the subject areas into daily tasks is similar to

____ a. specifying unit objectives.
____ b. making daily lesson plans.
____ c. both.
____ d. neither.

4. Materials collected to cover the instructional objectives must be evaluated for

____ a. correspondence to objectives.
____ b. quality of content.
____ c. both.
____ d. neither.

5. The final step in preparation of materials is

____ a. reorganization of the classroom.
____ b. placing reinforcing materials on the shelf.
____ c. assigning materials into task units.
____ d. constructing the RE menu.

6. The two basic types of diagnostic tests used in the contingency managed classroom are:

a. ______________________________
b. ______________________________

7. The main purpose(s) of the diagnostic test is (are)

____ a. to offer the teacher a basis for placement.
____ b. to check the quality of the materials.
____ c. both.
____ d. neither.

8. Two standardized tests which may be used for prescriptive purposes are

____ a. WAIS.
____ b. California Achievement Test.
____ c. Flanagan Aptitude Classification Test.
____ d. Stanford Achievement Test.

9. Which of these statements about diagnostic test materials is (are) true?

____ a. Prescriptive test items are prepared for course objectives.
____ b. Progress checks are prepared for items on daily task lists.
____ c. Both.
____ d. Neither.

8

Classroom organization

Reinforcing Events (REs) and RE Area.

In the contingency managed classroom, the teacher should provide the students with activities which they enjoy and which serve as reinforcers for students who have successfully completed their tasks. Perhaps the teacher may want to have the students bring REs from home. Also, the teacher should be able to identify "momentary REs" and make them contingent on a specific action of the student. Examples of momentary REs include going to get a drink, going to the locker, erasing the blackboard, etc. The student who asks if he might get a drink would be told to first finish his task and then go.

An important criterion for choosing REs in a classroom is whether the students can engage in them quietly rather than causing noise. Most teachers will probably prefer to choose REs that are quiet and that need not involve more than one student. Examples of relatively quiet REs corresponding to appropriate response levels for average age norms include:

REs for 3- to 5-year-olds

(1) Being read to
(2) Looking at books
(3) Playing with crayons
(4) Painting
(5) Working puzzles
(6) Cutting and pasting
(7) Playing with clay

REs for 6- to 8-year-olds

(1) Reading stories
(2) Playing with cards
(3) Drawing
(4) Painting
(5) Playing with tinker toys
(6) Playing dominoes
(7) Working puzzles

REs for 9- to 11-year-olds

(1) Reading comics
(2) Reading science fiction, mystery stories, etc.
(3) Working puzzles
(4) Playing chess
(5) Playing checkers
(6) Drawing
(7) Painting

REs for 12- to 14-year-olds

(1) Playing chess
(2) Playing cards
(3) Writing letters
(4) Reading magazines, books, comics
(5) Playing dominoes
(6) Talking
(7) Playing tic tac toe

REs for 15- to 16-year-olds

(1) Talking
(2) Playing tic tac toe
(3) Playing chess
(4) Reading books, magazines, comics
(5) Working jigsaw puzzles
(6) Playing checkers
(7) Writing letters

Figure 1
Sample RE Menu For Young Children

Ask the student to pick what he would like to do from this menu.

Obviously there are many overlapping REs from one age category to another. There are many other REs that could and should be included in a contingency managed classroom. The most important REs are those that are directly related to the educational objectives, and these should be high priority on any RE menu. Examples are discussions in groups with the teacher, roleplaying, viewing relevant motion pictures or filmstrips.

After having determined the REs that are available to the students, the teacher should make a reinforcing event "menu." The REs can be written or pictured on a large poster, bulletin board or something similar. (See Figure 1.) The menu should be placed adjacent to the RE area and made easily available to the students. To avoid a large cluster of students around the menu, the teacher might want to provide two menus and arrange for students from one-half of the class to use one and students from the other half to use the other.

Another problem which the teacher should control is a student's repeated selection of the same RE. The student becomes satiated with it after a while and it becomes less reinforcing. To control this, the teacher should arrange to change items on the menu periodically, and inform the students of the REs newly available.

Instructional Frames

1. An appropriate reinforcing event for the classroom may be one which (check all that apply)

____ a. offers opportunities to leave the classroom.
____ b. the student engages in before completing his task.
____ c. involves a toy brought from home.
____ d. involves other children in the activity.
____ e. makes considerable noise.

a, c, d

2. Select four reinforcing events that you believe would be effective with the students you teach. (Note: they may be quite different from the ones listed in the text.)

____
____
____
____

3. Is it desirable for an RE to be an activity which, in itself, fulfills an educational function?

   a. Yes
   b. No   a

Specification of Time Spent in RE Area

The teacher should establish a method for determining how long a student may stay in the RE area at a time. Students should probably not spend more than ten nor less than three minutes in the RE area as reward for each task. If more time is spent, the RE may lose its value as a reinforcer for completing tasks. If less than three minutes is allowed, the student doesn't have the opportunity to actually get involved in the RE before the time is up. The total RE period should be limited during any 50-minute class period. The criterion for determining the amount of time can be established in several ways. The teacher could correlate the amount of time with the difficulty of the task, i.e., the more difficult the task the longer the amount of time the student could spend in the RE. The teacher could determine the amount of time on a prespecified basis, i.e., RE time would always be five minutes. Another possibility would be to determine time on a varying schedule based on random selection of intervals of from three to eight minutes.

Methods of Controlling Time in RE Area

In addition to determining the amount of time the students may spend in the RE area, the teacher should have some means of assuring that the students are not spending more time than is allotted to them. Possible methods for controlling this factor are:

1. The use of sign-in/out sheets. Students would sign in, stating the time they begin, and sign out, stating the time they leave the area. The teacher could spot-check the sheets, and those students who have overstayed their time would be sent back to the task area.
2. In some cases, it might be possible to use time clocks or other timing devices. With time clocks, the buzzer would

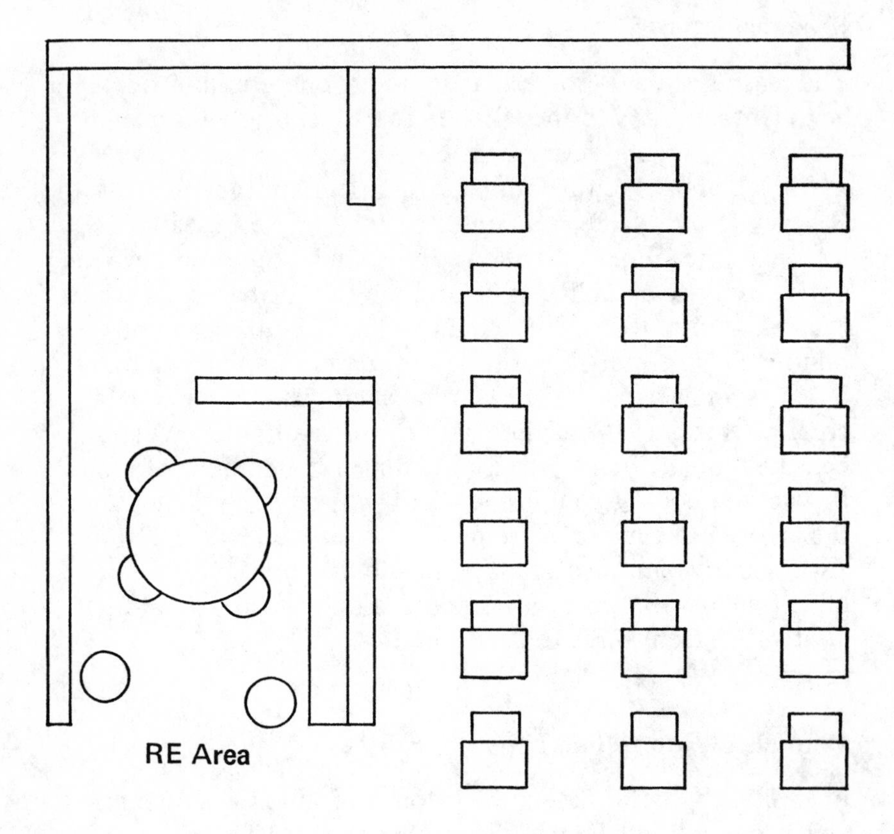

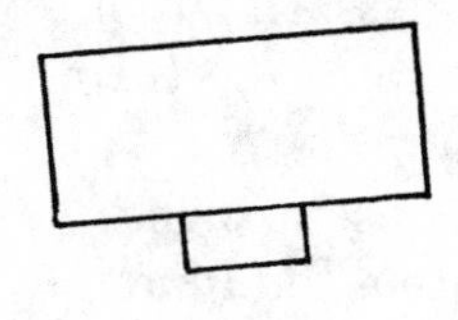

Figure 2
Sample Classroom Layout

sound at the end of the allotted period. This system is most easily implemented when there are few students in the class.

3. Students could be taught to leave the RE area each time the minute hand of the clock hit the number 1, 2, 3, etc. This method is convenient since each time the minute hand hits a given number, all the students would have to leave the RE area. It would cause the students to complete their tasks faster in order to have maximum time in the RE area.
4. Peer pressure can also be used. The students themselves will often remind others that time is up. When the teacher notices this occurring, he can send the overstaying student back to the task area. Students who consistently overstay can be controlled by being deprived of as much RE time as the overtime they already had, or by being told that their RE time is used up for several days.

Instructional Frames

1. Once the REs have been selected, they should be

____ a. listed on a menu.
____ b. checked to determine whether the students actually like them.
____ c. changed from time to time. — a, b, c

2. The length of time allowed in the RE area should be

____ a. no more than three minutes.
____ b. at least three minutes.
____ c. equal to the time the student spends on the task. — b

3. Once the length of time for an RE has been determined, the teacher should

____ a. not enforce the time limit very strictly.
____ b. allow students to estimate or guess when their times are up.
____ c. devise a method for limiting the time. — c

Preparing the RE Area and Task Area

The RE area is a place where the students engage in their REs. This area can be another room or an area separated from the task area in the same room. It is probably most effective to have students engaged in REs in an area separated in some way from those working on their assignments to control the amount of talking between the two groups. (See Figure 2, p. 88.) If this is not possible, students can engage in individual, quiet REs at their desks. In such a case the student has his individual RE menu. He also can be taught to signal that he is engaging in an RE by, for example, pinning a colored card to his clothes. In this manner, the teacher can easily determine when students are engaging in reinforcing activities. This signal system is also valuable when a separate RE area has been arranged.

A method of coping with the noise level generated in the RE area of a single room set-up is to play quiet background music. This serves to compete with and to mask the noise.

The task area should be designated as that location where the students work on their tasks. Students in this area should not be allowed to talk among themselves, and should not engage in external reinforcing events. The desks should be grouped so all students performing their tasks are in the same general area.

Organizing Materials

The teacher should organize instructional materials near the task area so they are easily accessible to the students. Materials should be organized by subject matter, e.g., multiplication, division, reading, history, etc. If the teacher is teaching only one subject, such as English, she would probably organize her materials by titles. Materials should also be organized by the diagnostic levels to which the teacher has assigned them.

To keep materials from becoming disorganized, it might be good for the teacher to assign different students the job of reorganization. This in itself might be used as an RE.

Instructional Frames

1. To avoid disturbing students who are working on tasks, the RE area should be

____ a. identical with the task area.
____ b. separated from the task area. b

2. Background music can provide a means of

____ a. letting students know that their RE periods are over.
____ b. giving reinforcements to students.
____ c. preventing RE noise from disturbing students working on tasks. c

3. Which of the following activities should *not* be permitted in the RE area?

____ a. Talking to other students
____ b. RE activities
____ c. Work on tasks c

4. Materials in the task area should be organized according to ______________ matter and according to level of ______________. subject, difficulty

Flowchart No. 2
RE Specifications (See Chapter 8)

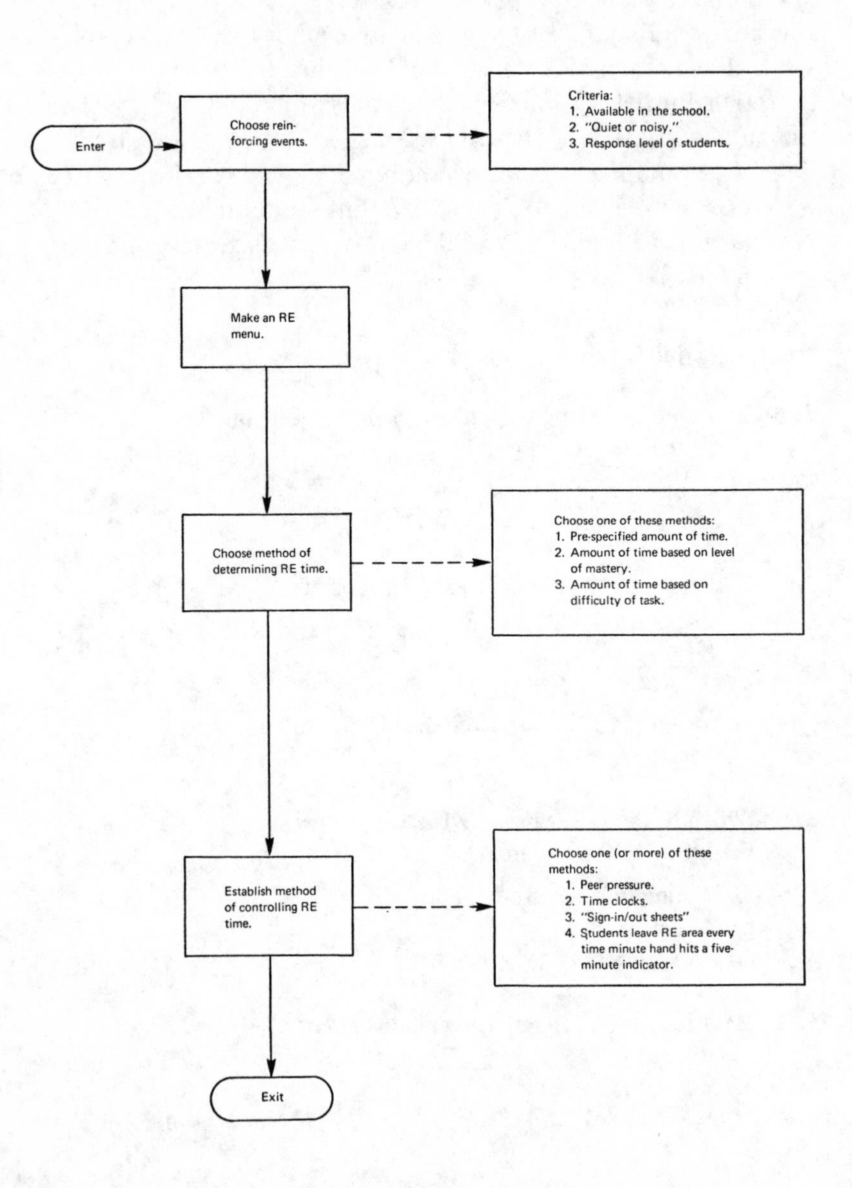

Post-test

1. In the RE area,

____ a. time spent should be no less than 15 minutes in each class hour.
____ b. the teacher specifies the number of tasks.
____ c. both.
____ d. neither.

2. The task area

____ a. must be physically in the same room as the RE area.
____ b. must be used only for work.
____ c. should contain the instructional materials.
____ d. all of these.
____ e. none of these.

3. RE time may be controlled by

____ a. sign-in/out sheets.
____ b. timer clocks.
____ c. peer pressure.
____ d. all of these.
____ e. none of these.

4. Reinforcing events should be chosen on the basis of

____ a. the size of the RE menu.
____ b. the number of objectives for the course.
____ c. both.
____ d. neither.

5. Which of these is an example of a momentary RE?

____ a. A student wants to get a drink.
____ b. A student wants to gaze out the window.
____ c. Both.
____ d. Neither.

Flowchart No. 3
Specification of Classroom Layout
(See Chapter 8)

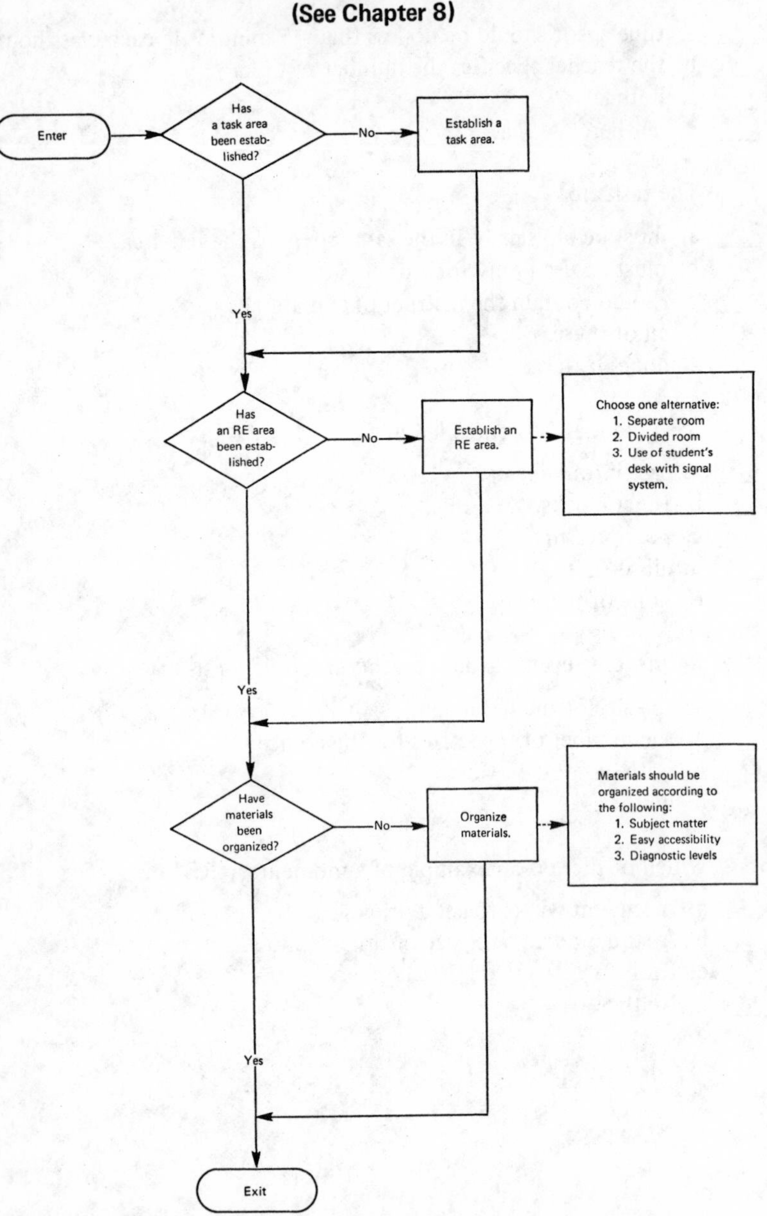

9

Management of the class

Orientation of Students

On the first day of class, students should be oriented to the contingency managed classroom. With older students the teacher may choose to explain first the relatively simple concept of "If you do X successfully, then you can have (do) Y." If the teacher feels it necessary, he should explain that doing X successfully involves a short test to determine if the student has learned the assigned information.

The students should understand the particular grading procedure the teacher has chosen and the consequences of not passing the progress check; i.e., that the consequences may be (a) an explanation by the teacher and retaking the progress check, or (b) doing the task again, or (c) doing another task and passing its progress check before receiving an RE.

Orientation Methods. Two possible methods for orienting the students are:

- The teacher can choose a student to be used as an example to the class, and take this student through the various stages of orientation. Having done this, the teacher can answer any questions and then let each of the students go through the process with individual assistance where needed.
- Each student may be oriented individually.

Orientation Procedures. An orientation flowchart has been developed (see page 97) using the concept of chaining. An example of chaining used as a training device is teaching a child to say "Washington" by saying "ton" first, then "ington," and finally "Washington." The teacher should apply the following steps to orientation for his own arrangement of areas, menus, etc.

1. Show the student the REs and explain the length of time he may spend in the RE area and the system for signalling when that time is over. Allow him to engage in an RE for a short time (one minute), and have him leave the area on signal.
2. Explain the RE menu, have the student choose an RE, and let him again have the RE.
3. Explain that when the student has successfully completed a progress check, this is the signal for going to the menu. After this, the teacher should say something like "All right, you passed your progress check, and now you may go to the menu."
4. After the student has again completed steps 3, 2, and 1, in that order, a task should be assigned. (At this point, students who can read should be introduced to the student record sheet, the diagnostic profile, and the daily assignments. The teacher would probably prefer to assign tasks orally to pre-readers or non-readers.) After the student has engaged in a task, he should take a progress check. On passing, the student should go to the menu, choose an RE, and engage in the RE for a short period. Now he has completed the orientation cycle.

The teacher may object to having the students engage in many REs during orientation. However, the experience in the RE area of doing something they enjoy, after successfully completing a task, makes them more eager to complete tasks rapidly in the future.

Flowchart No. 4
Orientation to Contingency Managed Classroom
(See Chapter 9)

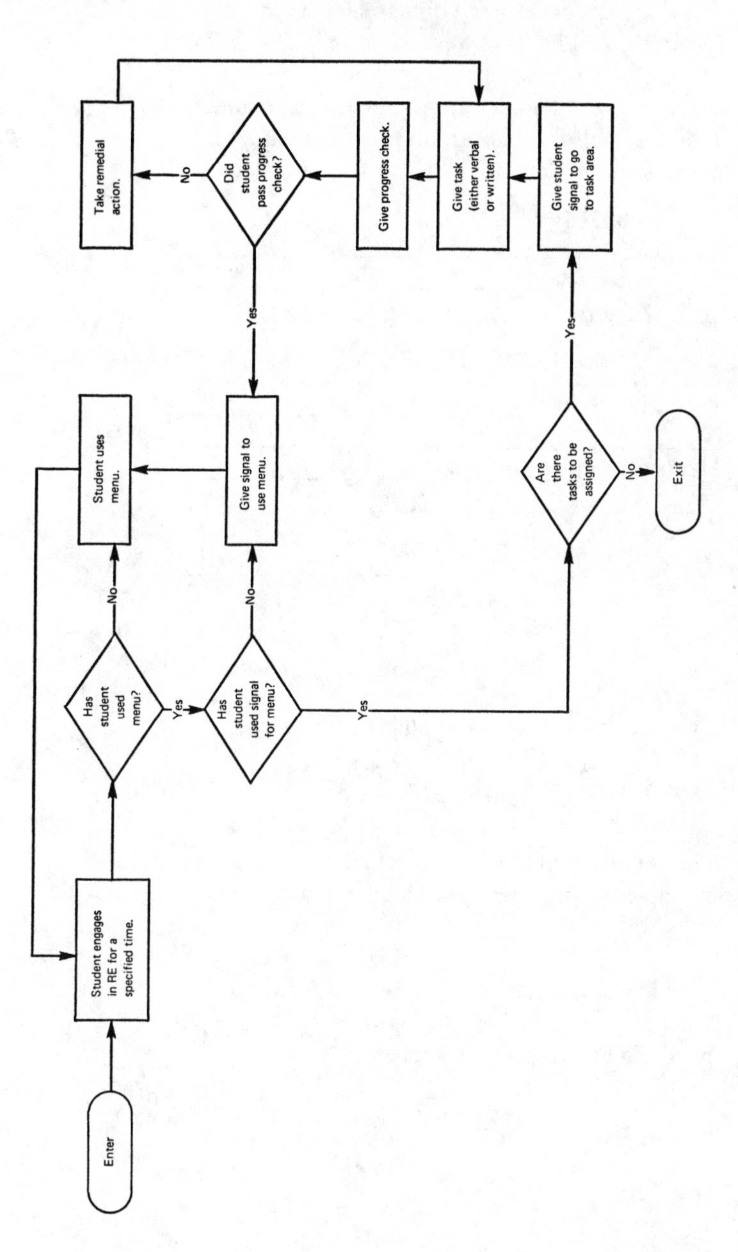
Enter
Student engages in RE for a specified time.
Has student used menu?
No
Student uses menu.
Yes
Has student used signal for menu?
No
Give signal to use menu.
Yes
Did student pass progress check?
No
Take remedial action.
Yes
Are there tasks to be assigned?
No
Exit
Yes
Give student signal to go to task area.
Give task (either verbal or written).
Give progress check.

Instructional Frames

1. Imagine a particular elementary or high school class. It may be a class you actually teach or have taught. Plan how you would explain each feature of a contingency management system listed below, in a way appropriate to the grade level and cultural background of your students. Write your explanations on the lines provided.

   The contract principle ______________________
   ____
   Prescriptive test ___________________________
   ____
   Task units _________________________________
   ____
   Progress checks ____________________________
   ____
   Menu of reinforcing events __________________
   ____
   Time limit on REs __________________________
   ____

   Answers will vary. They should not be overly detailed or complex.

2. "The vowels are a, e, i, o and u."
   "The vowels are a, e, i, o and__."
   "The vowels are a, e, i, __ and __."
   "The vowels are a, e, __, __ and __."

   The sequence of statements above is an example of the training device known as ____________________.

   chaining

3. In many cases, students will be involved in a large number of REs during the orientation period. This situation is probably

   ___ a. desirable.
   ___ b. undesirable.

   a

Prescriptive Procedures

Administering Prescriptive Test. In order to determine each student's achievement level, the teacher should administer the prescriptive test after student orientation has been completed.

The teacher can of course begin establishing contracts with the students during the testing period. Thus, simply completing a section of the test would be a combination task-and-progress-check. After a student had completed a specified section, he would be permitted to have an RE.

In addition to the information which the teacher can get from tests, it may be possible to talk to the student's previous teachers or to send a form (see Figure 1) to teachers from the previous year. Pertinent information of value to the teacher would include the student's attitudes toward school, his rate of progress through instructional materials, and his strengths and weaknesses in relevant subjects.

Student's Name ____________________

Evaluator's Name ____________________

Date: ____________________

	Excellent	Above Average	Average	Below Average	Poor
Attitudes toward school					
Conduct in the class					
Rate of progress through materials					
Areas of exceptional academic achievement	1. 2. 3.				
Areas of academic weakness	1. 2. 3.				

Figure 1

Identification of Problem Areas. The student should be informed of his test results. After areas of required additional instruction have been determined, the teacher should also note areas in which the student excels, emphasizing these to the student. Test items should be carefully examined to determine any inconsistency between a student's test score and actual knowledge. A test score, for example, may indicate that the student is generally excelling in spelling but is consistently misspelling certain words. A few hours of concentrated study can remedy the deficiency and bring the student's skill up to the desired level.

Another example is specifically related to grade scores attained on the Stanford Achievement Test for first grade students. It is conceivable that a first grader could achieve an overall grade score of 2.6 on the mathematics section, indicating that he is excelling in first grade mathematics. However, close examination might indicate that he is having problems in dealing with concepts of weight and measurement. Given this information, the teacher should prescribe instructional materials for the child dealing with the specific concepts of weight and measurement. After the student completed that instructional unit the teacher might find, through another prescriptive test, that the student was now responding on a level several months beyond the 2.6 first indicated.

If the diagnostic test shows the student strong in all parts of an area, he may be allowed to skip the instruction related to that area. If the student says he knows the material, this should be verified by the administration of appropriate progress checks. Any student who scores 90 percent correct, or above, may skip the material.

It is important to note that the student's areas of strength are probably (although not necessarily) the areas that he most enjoys working in. The best way to find out if the student enjoys working in an area is by asking him, and watching his behavior in class. Working on tasks related to strong areas may be used as reinforcing events for the student.

Recording Diagnostic Information. After the teacher carefully examines the prescriptive test and scores it, noting strengths and weaknesses, the results should be recorded on the

Figure 2
Sample Student Record Sheet

Student's Name ______________________________

Week of: ______________________________

DIAGNOSTIC PROFILE. Name of Test: ____________________

Day 1	Test Scores:	Specified Weaknesses:	Specified Strengths:
	1.	1.	1.
	2.	2.	2.
	3.	3.	3.
	4.	4.	4.
	5.	5.	5.
	Etc.	Etc.	Etc.
Day 2	Name of Task:	Materials:	Specified Amount:
	1. Adding Fractions	1. Trouble Shooting Mathematics Skills	1. p. 20, problems 1-6
	2. Comprehension	2. Reading for Understanding	2. p. 8, whole story
	3. Spelling "ie" Words	3. Assigned List of Words	3. 20 words
Day 3	Name of Task:	Materials:	Specified Amount:
	1. Adding Fractions	1. Trouble Shooting Mathematics Skills	1. p. 21, problems 1-6
	2. Comprehension	2. Reading for Understanding	2. p. 8, whole story
	3. Spelling "ie" words	3. Assigned List of Words	3. 20 words
Day 4	Name of Task:	Name of Task:	Name of Task:
	1. Adding Fractions	1. Trouble Shooting Mathematics Skills	1. p. 22, problems 1-6
	2. Comprehension	2. Reading for Understanding	2. p. 11, whole story
	3. Unit Test on "ie" Spelling Words	3. Unit Test	3. 20 words
Day 5	Name of Task:	Materials	Specified Amount:
	1. Unit Test on Adding Fractions	1. See Teacher for Test	1. 8 problems
	2. Comprehension	2. Reading for Understanding	2. p. 14, whole story
	3. Vocabulary—Define and Use in a Sentence	3. Vocabulary Cards	3. 10 cards

student's record sheet which will be kept in each student's folder. The format for recording the results could be as shown in Figure 2. The teacher may choose to record the scores, list the areas of weakness and strength, or both.

The criteria for making this decision would depend on the prescriptive test itself. If the test covers one specific skill, recording the score would be sufficient, but a prescriptive test might deal with a subject area that involves addition, subtraction, word problems, weights, measurements, etc. In this case, it would probably be necessary to record the overall score for arithmetic plus the specific areas of strength and weakness. When a standardized profile sheet is provided, specific areas of strength and weakness should still be isolated and recorded. See Flowchart No. 5.

Each time the teacher gives the student a prescriptive test, the information should be recorded on the student's record sheet. Being able to note his progress is an important source of reinforcement for the student. The teacher may also want it as her record of the test scores, weaknesses, strengths, and other personal information about the student.

Instructional Frames

1. The next step after orientation is administration of p____________________ t____________. — *prescriptive tests*

2. Which of the following practices are desirable during the testing stage?

____ a. Providing REs for completion of test sections
____ b. Letting a student know his test results
____ c. Using data from other sources to corroborate a student's test scores
____ d. Determining what learning activities a student finds desirable
____ e. Emphasizing a student's failures as much as his successes when talking to him
____ f. Recording precisely what skills the student has not mastered — *a, b, c, d, f*

Specification of Assignments

Identification of Diagnostic Level. It is necessary for the teacher to determine the level on which each student is responding regarding a subject area. This may be determined directly from the test scores themselves but, as previously mentioned, these scores often relate to gross subject areas.

The teacher can more accurately determine the diagnostic level of a student by examining the unit and daily tasks of the course, and deciding at what point they exceed the student's level of knowledge as shown by the test results.

Identification of Corresponding Task Materials. Having already determined what materials will be used, and having correlated these materials with the units of study, the teacher will specify for each student the materials appropriate to the student's diagnostic level.

Preparation of Individual Task List. After having determined the student's diagnostic level and the corresponding instructional materials, the teacher should record the information on the student's record sheet. Information recorded should specifically include the size of the tasks the student is to work on. This will be called a "task list." The size of the task may be a series of page numbers, or a specific chapter, or it may be "the first five sentences of the third paragraph on page 35." The tasks can be recorded by the teacher daily or by unit of instruction. Mature students possibly would be able to record their own daily tasks if the teacher has prepared a master plan of tasks necessary to complete a unit.

In addition to the results from the diagnostic test, the record sheet should include the daily assignments.

Establishing Daily Contracts

The essential elements of any contract are "If you do X, then you may have (do) Y," but the contracting procedure is more complex than that. It is graphically presented in Flowchart No. 6.

Flowchart No. 5
Diagnostics and Prescriptions (See Chapter 9)

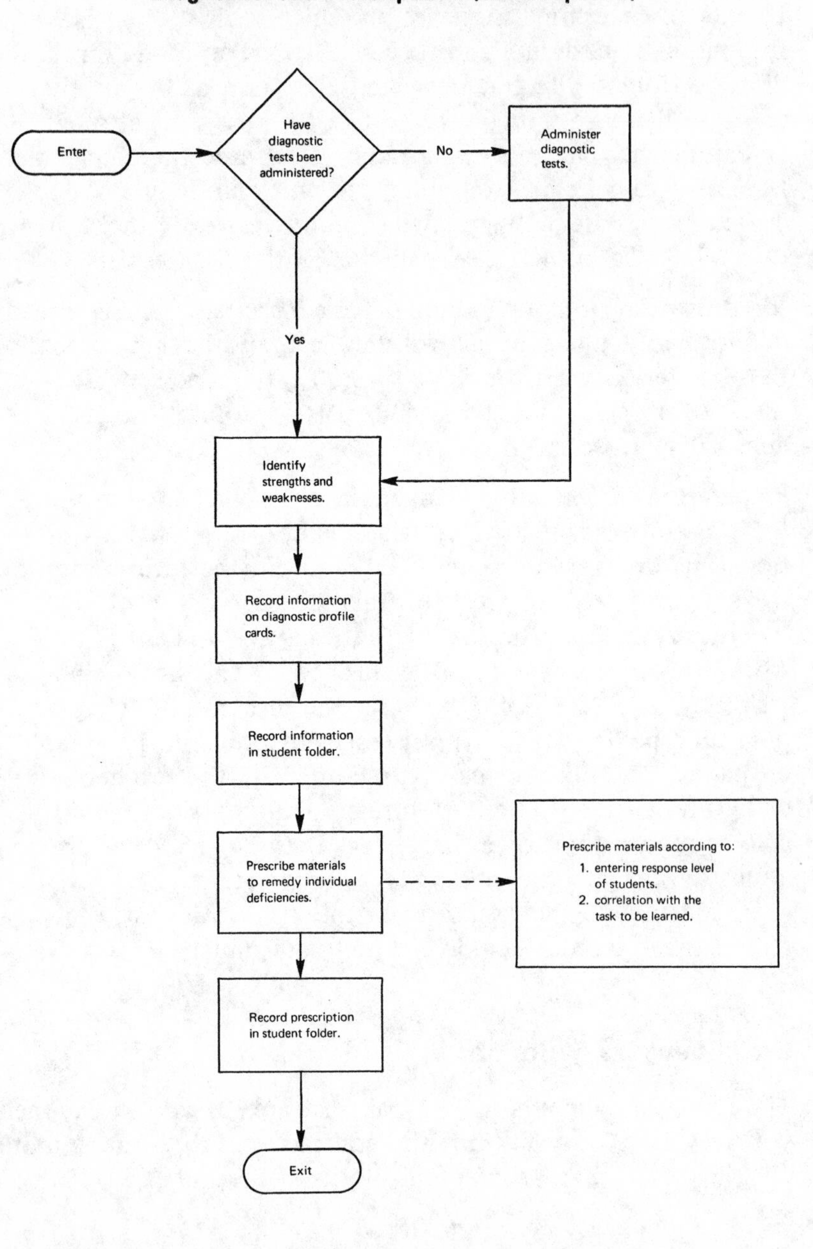

Flowchart No. 6
Specification of Contracting (See Chapter 9)

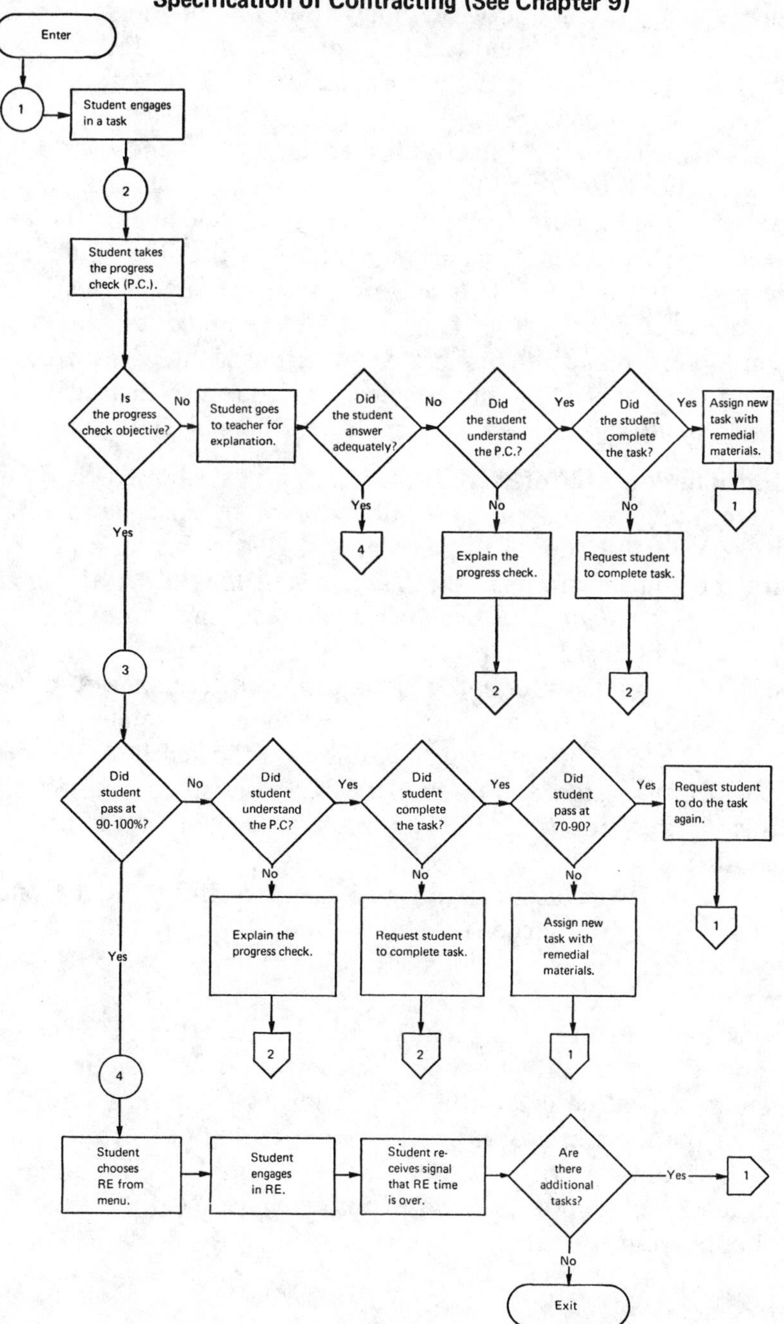

The Implicit Definition of the Contract. The contract is: a non-preferred task (a task which the student does not particularly enjoy doing and which may be in one of the student's areas of weakness); followed by a progress check; followed by a reinforcing event if the progress check is passed; if not, several alternatives are open as shown on the flowchart.

The student should not be forced to go over and over a task without any sort of break. If the student is making an effort without successfully completing his assignment, the teacher should administer a progress check that the student will be able to pass, and send him to the RE area. (This is because going to the RE area must always be contingent on some performance demonstrated by the student.) In such an event, it is likely that the diagnosis and the resulting task assignments should be re-examined and possibly altered.

Introduction of Preferred Tasks. After the system has been in effect long enough for the students to become accustomed to its concepts, it should be possible for the teacher to arrange for the students to engage in *tasks which they enjoy doing* as reinforcing events. For example, a student may thoroughly enjoy doing tasks which involve reading, but may intensely dislike doing his fractions. In this case, the teacher would have the student do his fractions, followed by a task related to reading. This reinforcing task would be followed by a progress check just as are non-preferred tasks. If the student passes this progress check successfully, he would then engage in another low-preference task.

The teacher must remember to reinforce the student from time to time for successful completion of a preferred task—orally, verbally or by allowing him to progress to the RE menu.

If the student has difficulty with the preferred task and cannot pass the progress check successfully the first time, it is best to follow successful completion of the task with an RE from the menu. Also, if specified reinforcing tasks cannot be defined for a particular student, the teacher should continue to reinforce each successfully completed task with an RE chosen from the menu.

Instructional Frames

1. In determining the exact diagnostic level of a student, the teacher will probably have to refer to

____ a. the actual unit tasks of the course.
____ b. the student's test scores.
____ c. the student's preferences on the RE menu. — a and b

2. A task list is a record of

____ a. the student's behavior characteristics.
____ b. specific instructional assignments for an individual student.
____ c. items of information which every student in the class must cover in a given time period. — b

3. Which of the following statements best describes the policy the teacher should follow in dealing with students who do not consistently complete tasks in a satisfactory manner?

____ a. A student should be consistently required to repeat a task until he masters it.
____ b. If a student fails at a task occasionally, he should be given an RE anyway, to reward his effort.
____ c. The teacher should alter the tasks, if necessary to bring about some degree of success, and provide an RE only after some instance of satisfactory performance.
____ d. If the tasks have been correctly defined in the first place, no changes should be necessary for individual students. — c

4. If a teacher discovers that a particular kind of learning task is one the student enjoys, it may be desirable to

____ a. omit the task from the program.
____ b. make the task an RE.
____ c. omit progress checks for that task.
____ d. avoid providing REs for performance of that task. — b

Post-test

1. Prescriptive tests should be administered

____ a. after students have been oriented to the contingency managed classroom.
____ b. after explaining the test to the students.
____ c. in conjunction with collecting other possible information regarding the student.
____ d. all of these.
____ e. none of these.

2. If the prescriptive test shows that the student scores at the 90 percent correct level in a specific area, he

____ a. may get an RE before he does his task.
____ b. may skip the corresponding set of tasks.
____ c. both.
____ d. neither.

3. Prescriptive information should be recorded

____ a. in the students' task lists.
____ b. in terms of overall scores and specific areas of strengths and weaknesses.
____ c. both.
____ d. neither.

4. With respect to each task, the student's record sheet should contain:

a. ____
b. ____
c. ____

5. Having determined the student's prescriptive test scores, the teacher should

____ a. check its relation to the instructional objectives.
____ b. determine what the student's next task assignments should be.
____ c. identify the task materials which correspond to this score.
____ d. all of these.
____ e. none of these.

6. The contract stated in its most simple form is: ________________
____

7. The contract as defined above implicitly consists of a ____________, followed by a _________________________, followed by an _________________________ .

8. Decisions which the teacher must make after the student has taken a progress check include

____ a. whether the student should go to the RE area before the progress check is graded.
____ b. whether the student has successfully passed the progress check.
____ c. both.
____ d. neither.

9. If the student did not pass the progress check, the teacher has several courses of action open, including

____ a. having the student go to the RE area while the teacher determines his specific weakness.
____ b. having the student go on to the next unit.
____ c. both.
____ d. neither.

10. If the teacher finds that the student has tried very hard to complete a task successfully, but seems unable to do so after two or three tries,

____ a. the student should be given an easier task whose progress check he can pass.
____ b. the student should repeat the task.
____ c. both.
____ d. neither.

11. Which tasks can be used as reinforcing events?

____ a. Those tasks in which the student expresses interest.
____ b. Those tasks with which the student has most difficulty.
____ c. Both.
____ d. Neither.

12. Tasks used as reinforcing events should

____ a. be considered unimportant tasks.
____ b. require no progress checks.
____ c. both.
____ d. neither.

13. The basic principle in the procedure for orienting the students to the contingency managed classroom is

____ a. contract malfunction.
____ b. chaining.
____ c. individualized instruction.

14. In orientation, the teacher may

____ a. choose one student as an example in a group demonstration.
____ b. orient each student individually.
____ c. both of these.
____ d. neither of these.

15. The sequence of steps in orientation is

____ a. task + progress check + menu + RE.
____ b. RE + (Menu + RE) + (Task + progress check + menu + RE).
____ c. both.
____ d. neither.

10

Correcting contract malfunctions

Recognizing Malfunctions

A student fails in the classroom because the motivational system fails, not because the student is "stupid" or "bad." The teacher should note how each student is responding to the contingency contracting system. When one or more of the following symptoms is observed, the contract should be revised or altered.

1. Unfinished assignments
2. Complaining
3. Excessive dawdling
4. Talking and wasting time
5. Looking at the clock excessively
6. Inattention to instructions or details
7. Failure to pass more than two progress checks in one subject area

Students exhibiting any of the above-listed behaviors probably require special attention, and their contracts should be adjusted.

Methods of Remedying Malfunctions: Revising the Contract.

There are two ways of revising the contract–it can be lengthened or shortened, depending on the teacher's diagnosis of its malfunction.

Lengthening the Contract. When the student finishes all of his tasks before the expected time, the contract is probably too short. The student should receive the full benefit of the extra free time as a reinforcement for finishing his contract, but on the next day the contract may be lengthened by adding more tasks and REs. The student should be made to feel that this is reinforcing and that he has achieved a new status.

Of course, the same effect can be achieved by making the tasks within the contract more difficult, as by adding more tasks on the same level.

Shortening the Contract. When the student consistently fails to finish his contract for the day in the allotted time, the contract should be shortened. Tasks should be gradually and systematically deleted from each of the subject areas. Or the tasks within the contract can be simplified.

If this system is not successful, the teacher is probably not using the REs most appealing to that particular student. The situation then should be re-examined, and REs should be introduced that will motivate the student to finish his contract in the allotted time.

Instructional Frames

1. Freddy is a fifth grader whose teacher has placed the class on a contingency contracting system. Instead of reading his social studies tasks attentively, he pauses after reading for a few minutes, gazes out the window, then begins drawing pictures on a scrap of paper. Freddy continues this and similar behavior for several days. The problem is probably that

____ a. Freddy has a personality problem.
____ b. contingency contracting simply will not work with certain children.
____ c. the terms of the contract are not appropriate for Freddy.

c

2. Freddy's teacher should try to deal with the problem by

____ a. giving up contingency contracting in the class.
____ b. adjusting the length of his tasks.
____ c. scolding Freddy for his misbehavior.
____ d. selecting a different social studies textbook. b

3. List some kinds of student behavior that might indicate something is wrong with the contract:

____
____
____
____ See p. 111

4. If a student works faster than the teacher anticipated and completes tasks rapidly, the length or difficulty of the tasks should probably be

____ a. increased.
____ b. decreased.
____ c. left the same until the RE is adjusted. a

Conclusion

Instruction and motivation are two equally essential components of any educational system. During the past few years teachers have begun to understand the tremendous importance of defining educational objectives in precise behavioral terms. Recent progress in educational technology has aided teachers in defining these objectives. Technological breakthroughs have also made it possible to obtain self-instructional materials which are based on, and correspond to, well-defined objectives.

Motivation technology in the form of contingency management has been the primary concern of this book. More specifically, this book has explained how a teacher can apply modern motivation management techniques to improve the student's chances of succeeding in any subject area. Such improvements are especially significant in those areas where the student's motivation is relatively low because of lack of adequate preparation, a history of failure to obtain reinforcing consequences for his effort, or a failure on the part of previous teachers to use adequate motivation to facilitate academic performance and learning.

The techniques presented in this course may be summarized as follows:

1. **Objectives** of all educational activities must be clearly defined, specifying what the student should be able to do upon completion of a particular course or unit of instruction.

2. **Materials** corresponding to these objectives, whether they are in the form of texts, workbooks, lectures, experiments, or whatever, must also be clearly specified.

3. **Diagnostic tests** must be either obtained or prepared to measure the knowledge of the student at the time he is starting the program (prescriptive tests), as well as at the end of each bit of academic performance (progress checks).

4. **Events** which are **reinforcing** to each individual student must be assessed and made available as rewards for successful performance. Once all of the above steps have been established, and areas in which the student shows specific weaknesses have been determined, instructional materials must be secured, assigned, and contracted. RE menus, task and RE areas, diagnostic tests, and student task lists are all tools designed to facilitate the teacher's role as a motivation manager in the classroom. Equipped with these tools and with others, such as programed instruction courses, audio-visual aids, automated teaching machines, and other devices, today's teacher is ready to convert yesterday's mass education of students into tomorrow's individualized education.

Post-test

1. List five symptoms of a contract malfunction:

a. ______________________________

b. ______________________________

c. ______________________________

d. ______________________________

e. ______________________________

2. The two methods of correcting contract malfunctions are:

   a. ____
   b. ____

Criterion Test for Part II

Directions: In each multiple-choice question, choose one or more correct answers, except where "choose one" is indicated.

1. The steps required in the preparation of task materials for the contingency managed classroom are

a. Identification of the ________________ areas.
b. Breakdown of objectives into daily _______ ___________.
c. Collection of _________________ for subject areas.
d. Assignment of _____________ into ___________ units.

2. We are told that the course curriculum should be examined in terms of behavioral objectives. This means that

____ a. undesirable student behaviors are listed so they can more easily be avoided.
____ b. specific tasks can be identified to correct specific weaknesses.
____ c. when you know what you expect of your students, you are ready to teach it to them.
____ d. you should break the prescribed curriculum into daily task units, which all students will do together.
____ e. task units are more easily correlated with test items.

3. Ideally, in any one class period, the average student should complete

____ a. at least five task unit assignments, with at least two RE periods.
____ b. no more than one task unit, and one RE period.
____ c. at least two task units, and up to five RE periods.
____ d. two or three task units, each followed by an RE period.

4. Define a prescriptive test.

5. Define a progress check.

6. "Both momentary REs and REs a student brings from home should be ignored when planning reinforcement for student behavior." This statement is (choose one)

____ a. true.
____ b. false.
____ c. partly true.

7. The best REs are those that (choose one)

____ a. the student chooses from a menu.
____ b. involve big-muscle activity.
____ c. are active rather than passive.
____ d. are educational.
____ e. do not require much effort or concentration.

8. It is suggested that the best way to orient students to the contingency contracting system is by means of chaining. This means

____ a. the same as "first work, then play."
____ b. that they practice the last event in the series first.
____ c. that the students take turns going through the steps.
____ d. the same as Grandma's Law.

9. In prescribing tasks for a given student, the teacher should rely on data from

____ a. general intelligence tests.
____ b. general achievement tests.
____ c. general aptitude tests.
____ d. specific subject matter tests.
____ e. previous teachers.
____ f. performance on progress checks.

10. If a student fails more than once on a particular progress check, his teacher should

____ a. coach him personally on troublesome parts of the test.
____ b. send him to the RE area for a break before having him try again.
____ c. assign him an easier task, for which he can be rewarded.
____ d. skip that progress check and give him his next task assignment.

11. When a student finishes all his assigned daily tasks well before the expected time,

____ a. he should be rewarded for his conscientiousness with extra time in the RE area.
____ b. his contract should be lengthened.
____ c. his contract should be shortened.
____ d. he should be given review work.

Match your answers against the answers given on page 130.

ANSWERS

Chapter 1

Pretest	1. a
	2. a, b
	3. neither

If all of your answers to the pretest match those given, go to the post-test of this chapter. Otherwise, continue with the summary.

Intermediate Test	1. Positive
	2. Negative
	3. Negative

If all of your answers to the intermediate test match those given, go to the post-test of this chapter. Otherwise, continue with the frame sequence.

Post-test	1. a
	2. b
	3. both

If all of your answers to the post-test match those given, go to the pretest of Chapter 2. Otherwise, if you covered only the pretest, read the summary in *this* chapter. If you have already read the summary, go to the frame sequence. If you have already read both the summary and the frame sequence, review the frame sequence before going on to the next chapter.

Chapter 2

Pretest

1. both
2. a, b
3. all of these

If all of your answers to the pretest match those given, go to the post-test of this chapter. Otherwise, continue with the summary.

Intermediate Test

1. both
2. b
3. a
4. events

If all of your answers to the intermediate test match those given, go to the post-test of this chapter. Otherwise, continue with the frame sequence.

Post-test

1. a, b
2. reinforcer or reinforcing event
3. response
4. stimulus

If all of your answers to the post-test match those given, go to the pretest of Chapter 3. Otherwise, if you covered only the pretest, read the summary in *this* chapter. If you have already read the summary, go to the frame sequence. If you have already read both the summary and the frame sequence, review the frame sequence before going on to the next chapter.

Chapter 3

Pretest
1. a, b, c, e, g
2. b, d, f, g, i

If all of your answers to the pretest match those given, go to the post-test of this chapter. Otherwise, continue with the summary.

Intermediate Test
1. all
2. b
3. all

If all of your answers to the intermediate test match those given, go to the post-test of this chapter. Otherwise, continue with the frame sequence.

Post-test
1. a. fair,
   b. clear,
   c. honest,
   d. positive,
   e. systematic
   (in any order)
2. a. for accomplishment,
   b. for small approximations,
   c. (immediately) after the performance,
   d. frequently (with small amounts),
   e. immediately
   (in any order)

If all of your answers to the post-test match those given, go to the pretest of Chapter 4. Otherwise, if you covered only the pretest, read the summary in *this* chapter. If you have already read the summary, go to the frame sequence. If you have already read both the summary and the frame sequence, review the frame sequence before going on to the next chapter.

Chapter 4

Pretest

1. a, b
2. c
3. all of these
4. all of these
5. both
6. b

If all of your answers to the pretest match those given, go to the post-test of this chapter. Otherwise, continue with the summary.

Intermediate Test

1. b, c, d
2. none
3. b
4. a
5. a

If all of your answers to the intermediate test match those given, go to the post-test of this chapter. Otherwise, continue with the frame sequence.

Post-test

1. b
2. b
3. both of these
4. b
5. a. task
   b. menu
   c. contract
6. a. task
   b. termination (completion, etc.)
   c. criteria

If all of your answers to the post-test match those given, go to the pretest of Chapter 5. Otherwise, if you covered only the pretest, read the summary in *this* chapter. If you have already read the summary, go to the frame sequence. If you have already read both the summary and the frame sequence, review the frame sequence before going on to the next chapter.

Chapter 5

Pretest

1. both
2. any of these
3. manager
4. student
5. a. manager
   b. student
6. c
7. micro-contracts

If all of your answers to the pretest match those given, go to the post-test of this chapter. Otherwise, continue with the summary.

Intermediate Test

1. a, b, c, e
2. all of these
3. c
4. any of these
5. d
6. micro-contracts
7. b

If all of your answers to the intermediate test match those given, go to the post-test of this chapter. Otherwise, continue with the frame sequence.

Post-test

1. Level 1. Manager-controlled contracting. Both the task and the reinforcement are determined by the manager alone.
   Level 2. Transitional step 1. Partial involvement of the student. The student participates in determining *either* the amount of reinforcement *or* the amount of task, *but not both.*
   Level 3. Transitional step 2. Equal control by manager and student. Full determination of *either* the reinforcement *or* the task by the student, *but not both; or* partial determination of both the task and the reinforcement by the student.
   Level 4. Transitional step 3. Partial involvement of the manager in the determination of either the task or the reinforcement. The other term is fully determined by the student.
   Level 5. Student-controlled contracting. Full determination of both the task and the reinforcement by the student.
2. macro

If all of your answers to the post-test match those given, go to the pretest of Chapter 6. Otherwise, if you covered only the pretest, read the summary in *this* chapter. If you have already read the summary, go to the frame sequence. If you have already read both the summary and the frame sequence, review the frame sequence before going on to the next chapter

Criterion Test for Part I—Answers

1. b (Chapter 1)
2. negative (Chapter 1)
3. a. it must be something highly desirable to the student.
   b. it must be something unobtainable without performing the task.
   (either order) (Chapter 2)
4. reinforcer or reinforcing event (Chapter 2)
5.

Contracting must be:	The contract should reward:
a. fair.	f. accomplishment.
b. clear.	g. small approximations.
c. honest.	h. after the performance.
d. positive.	i. frequently.
e. systematic.	j. immediately.
(in any order)	(in any order) (Chapter 3)

6. a. reinforce
   b. be reinforced (Chapter 3)
7. The answer should include mention of:
   a. individual task assignments.
   b. reinforcement list (menu).
   c. presentation and acceptance of the contract.
   d. performance of the task to criterion.
   e. delivery of the reinforcement as specified (Chapter 4).
8. a. the amount of the task
   b. the amount of the reinforcement
   c. the signals indicating the beginning and the termination of the task and the reinforcement (in any order) (Chapter 4)
9. b, c
10. A macro-contract is a contingency contract in which the task is the performance of a number of micro-contracts (or one in which performance under micro-contracts is reinforced by a specific reward).
11. A micro-contract is a contingency contract in which the only reinforcement is the reward specified in the contract itself.
12. A transitional contract is a contingency contract in which the student participates in the determination of either the amount of task, or the amount of reinforcement, or both. (Chapter 5)
13. No, such a macro-contract would not satisfy the rules of contracting as presented in this course. (Chapters 3 & 5)
14. Yes, if it becomes more desirable to the student than another task, and if it is used as a reinforcer for the performance of that other task. (Chapters 2, 3, 4)

15. Level 1. Manager-controlled contracting. Both the task and the reinforcement are determined by the manager alone.

Level 2. Transitional step 1–Partial involvement of the student. The student participates in determining *either* the amount of reinforcement *or* the amount of task, *but not both.*

Level 3. Transitional step 2–Equal control by manager and student. Full determination of *either* the reinforcement *or* the task by the student, *but not both; or* partial determination of both the task and the reinforcement by the student.

Level 4. Transitional step 3–Partial involvement of the manager in the determination of either the task or the reinforcement. The other term is fully determined by the student.

Level 5. Student-controlled contracting. Full determination of both the task and the reinforcement by the student. (Chapter 5)

Chapter 7

1. d
2. c
3. b
4. c
5. c
6. prescriptive tests and
   progress checks (either order)
7. a
8. b, d
9. c

Chapter 8

1. d
2. c
3. d
4. d
5. c

Chapter 9

1. d
2. b
3. c
4. (a) name of task
   (b) materials
   (c) specified amount
5. d
6. "If you do X then you may have (do) Y."
7. task, progress check, RE
8. b
9. d
10. a
11. a
12. d
13. b
14. c
15. b

Chapter 10

1. Any five of the following:
   a. unfinished assignments
   b. complaining
   c. excessive dawdling
   d. talking and wasting time
   e. looking at the clock excessively
   f. inattention to instructions or details
   g. failure to pass more than two progress checks in a specific subject area
2. a. lengthening the contract
   b. shortening the contract

Criterion Test for Part II—Answers

1. a. subject
   b. task units
   c. materials
   d. materials, task (chapter 7)
2. b, c, e
3. d
4. Device for diagnosing and prescribing task areas to correct specific weaknesses.
5. Device for determining whether student has completed his task and learned the information it contained; whether he has earned his RE (chapter 7).
6. b (chapter 8)
7. d (chapter 8)
8. b (chapter 9)
9. b, d, e, f (chapter 9)
10. c (chapter 9)
11. b (chapter 10)